D1570893

SLIDE!

The Baseball Tragicomedy That Defined Me, My Family,
and the City of Philadelphia—
And How It All Could Have Been Avoided Had Someone Just
Listened to My Lesbian Great Aunt

CARL WOLFSON

www.mascotbooks.com

Slide! The Baseball Tragicomedy That Defined Me, My Family, and the City of Philadelphia—And How It All Could Have Been Avoided Had Someone Just Listened to My Lesbian Great Aunt

For more information, please contact:
Mascot Books
620 Herndon Parkway #320
Herndon, VA 20170
info@mascotbooks.com

Library of Congress Control Number: 2017913656

CPSIA Code: PBANG1017A
ISBN-13: 978-1-68401-568-9

Book Design by Ricky Frame

Printed in the United States

For Gary Thill, a great leftfielder

TABLE OF CONTENTS

September 21, 1964
12:25 a.m.

Our heroes returned from their 10-game road trip with a record of 90-60, with 12 to play. No Phillies team since the turn of the century had won more than 91.

An exuberant crowd began filling the concourse at Philadelphia International Airport early in the evening and swelled into the thousands by half past midnight. A local band sparked the revelers, who broke into cheers as they spotted Jim Bunning, Johnny Callison, and Richie Allen. A cordon of Philadelphia's finest held back the throng as Mayor James H. J. Tate rushed to hug the boys and officially welcome manager Gene Mauch.

The mayor captured the moment with a child's heart: "I'm hoping the pennant will be safe in Philadelphia by the weekend!"

CHICO RUIZ

National League Standings Morning of September 21, 1964				
TEAM	WINS	LOSSES	PCT.	G.B.
Philadelphia	90	60	.600	--
Cincinnati	83	66	.557	6.5
St. Louis	83	66	.557	6.5
San Francisco	83	67	.553	7
Milwaukee	77	72	.517	12.5
Pittsburgh	76	72	.514	13
Los Angeles	75	75	.500	15
Chicago	67	82	.450	22.5
Houston	63	88	.417	27.5
New York	50	99	.336	39.5

One run can decide a game. It can also haunt you for a lifetime. Dad had a hunch about it; in fact later he would call it a premonition. And who, in Philadelphia at least, wouldn't have believed him?

Five innings before, when we claimed our place behind the first-base boxes, he was ebullient. "Can't get better seats than these!" he told my sister in a voice just loud enough to be heard by strangers. "It pays to have contacts."

However he got the tickets, I was happy to be in Connie Mack Stadium on this cool and breezy September night. The smell of cigars and freshly poured beer, the strange tattoos on even stranger men who hawked dogs from steaming-hot tins seemed an exotic escape from my split-level suburban home where dusty liquor bottles were hidden deep in the credenza and an 11-year-old boy such as myself was told to turn his head when ladies' "unmentionables" were unwrapped on Christmas morning.

I had been to the ballpark a half dozen times, but the mood was never this upbeat, this communal. A groundskeeper leveling the infield danced and waved to fans in the bright red seats of the upper deck. Byrum Saam's cheery pre-game seemed to flow from a thousand transistor radios. People connected with the talk of destiny. Since April, a cast of unlikely names—Allen, Callison, Bunning, Short, Rojas—had defied logic and expectation and put all of us at the center of the baseball universe. In a few days, our Phillies would be National League champions. And in two weeks, the 1964 World Series would open right here.

With the Phils holding a 6 1/2-game lead with just 12 games to go, nothing was left but pesky math—the sure and steady reduction of our magic number from 7 to 0.

It was clear that the spirit had gripped Linda and Dad as well. Linda, whose reaction to outdoor activity approximated that of a cat dropped into a tub of water, gladly opened her program to score the game. My 14-year-old sister was pretty, but perpetually unhealthy. With allergies and asthma, she retreated to her room, where she engaged in bookish pursuits, often took meals, and prompted an endless family debate as to whether she required a humidifier or dehumidifier. Now, in the evening air, she was busy filling her scorecard with the names of the visiting Cincinnati Reds, listed by number on the colossal Ballantine Beer scoreboard in right center.

Then I witnessed another miracle. Dad stood next to an ice cream vendor with his wallet open. Grams, my mother's mother, once claimed Dad was so cheap he invented the limbo trying to get into a pay toilet. When we dined out, it was ALL YOU CAN EAT! When we left a motel at the shore, it was ALL THE ROOM TOWELS YOU CAN SWIPE! "They expect you to take them," he would insist. "They plan for that."

Our ballpark routine was always the same.

"Peanuts?"

"Hey! There's Peanuts Lowrey in the dugout!"

"Hot dogs?"

"The only hot dogs here are *those umps!*"

Short of Commissioner Ford Frick appearing to name us "Fans of the Year" and offer a lifetime supply of soft pretzels, there would be no snacks until the seventh-inning stretch. That's when Dad would finally calculate the evening's outlay: a quarter toll for the Ben Franklin Bridge, another quarter for the return trip, and one dollar protection money for our car. The latter was dispensed to two neighborhood boys who received a friendly deal from Dad: "Two quarters up front. And two more if I get back and still have four tires!" If the tickets were free, as they usually were, and he'd spent two dollars or less, we could eat.

Tonight, though, there had been no bridge toll or protection money. Mom had pronounced the stadium neighborhood "unsafe," and we had taken an excursion bus from South Jersey to North Philly. Having watched Dad spring for three bus tickets and lavish us with treats *before* the game, I settled in thinking life couldn't be much cooler. He even bought me a pennant that read: "Phillies—National League Champions 1964."

For five innings the teams were scoreless. I was typically bouncy and my mind wandered. I watched the motion of dancing moths in the great lights that towered over us. I raised my binoculars to the broadcast booth and found Richie Ashburn, who had spoken at our church's father-son dinner and whose stories of the hapless '62 Mets made us laugh so hard the pastor farted.

I glanced at the perfect penmanship on Linda's scorecard and thought about the box score I would clip from tomorrow's paper and paste into a tan-colored scrapbook that would then contain 151 box scores, all in order, and be placed on a bookshelf next to Dracula, The Mummy, and my other monster models.

With one out in the top of the sixth, Chico Ruiz stepped in to face Art Mahaffey. Ruiz was the Reds' rookie utility man. Mahaffey was fourth in our rotation behind Jim Bunning, Chris Short, and Dennis Bennett. I also knew him as my great Aunt Nelle's least-favorite Phil.

Aunt Nelle, now 79, was the reigning baseball authority in our family. She was a fan to the core and a bull of a woman who had little use for the delicately turned phrase. When a player (or manager) crossed her, she was relentless in her derision, which often manifested itself in the sly reworking of their names. "Ma-HALF-y" became "Ma-HEY-fey." One muff by shortstop Bobby Wine crowned him "Bobby Wino." And Tony Taylor, who crossed himself before each bat, was known as "The Pope."

When Ruiz singled to right, I knew it would send my crabby great aunt straight to her typewriter to peck out a letter that would contain absolutely no opening pleasantries:

Dear Carl,

That blind bozo Mahaffey couldn't find a strike zone if he were president of the Teamsters. His mother must have fed him on the floor, for he sure doesn't know what a plate is. I have half a mind to make a carbon copy of this letter and send it to the Phillies "brass" at Shibe Park. If they don't trade that lazy so-and-so to the lowly Cubs, they will surely have one less fan here in Harrisburg. I might just turn my allegiance to the Pirates and their Irish skipper, Danny Murtaugh, who knows how to handle a pitch-

*ing staff and would never allow that limp arm Mahaffey to
"grace" his mound at Forbes Field. Be polite and respectful
to your parents.*

The Old Battle-Ax Nelle

Aunt Nelle wrote regularly, with swift analysis of the Phillies and keen interest in my Little League career, which ended mercifully after one season playing third for my Oaklyn, New Jersey, team. "Holding down the old hot corner?" she would write. "You are sure to make your old, white-haired aunt proud!" I prayed nightly that she didn't unearth the truth.

In the field, I was a prepositional disaster: Balls went over, under, around, and through me. At the plate, I managed three hits all season. My abysmal efforts on defense and offense were surpassed in laughable rottenness only by my lack of speed, which soon earned me the league-wide nickname "Lead Bottom." In my most famous at-bat, I hit a ball that rolled all the way to the right field fence—a sure double or possible triple. The outfielder picked it up and threw me out at first.

At all times, I avoided eye contact with the crowd. I could only imagine Mom and Dad smiling gamely through the savage whispers.

"Those are Lead Bottom's parents!"

"Yeah. I heard when they dated it took him a year to get to first base."

My saving grace was the rest of the team, whose level of play only slightly exceeded mine. We won *one* game, after which the coach treated us to pizza. Dad climbed down from the bleachers and joined in the celebration. Later, I heard the dugout towels were missing.

Pilfering linen was far from Dad's mind now, with Ruiz on first. Vada Pinson lined the ball to right center, but Johnny Callison scooped it up and nailed him at second for out number two. As Ruiz moved to third, Dad leaned forward.

He had a handsome face, full and healthy, and light brown hair that, after 47 years, had begun to thin. It was his rich blue eyes, though, that always tipped me off to his frequent fears. About now, I expected him to be worried about missing the bus home, or if the game went into extra innings, how late Linda and I could stay up on a school night. Instead, he was transfixed on Ruiz.

As the dangerous Frank Robinson stepped in, I wished my old man out of his trance. "Do you think we'll walk him?"

It was unusual for Dad *not* to have an opinion.

"Do you think we'll walk him?"

Dad turned to me. "He's coming home!"

And, sure enough, Ruiz exploded off third to the gasps of 20,000 fans. Mahaffey, in full windup, seemed paralyzed.

Throw the ball! Throw the ball!

After a God-awful spell, Mahaffey threw wildly as Ruiz's right foot touched the plate. No one could believe it. A fan behind me cursed, and I learned Jesus' middle initial. Dad stood with his hands on his head. Linda sucked air. And I could only think of how freak-ish *we* must have looked. I imagined a four-column photo in the *Evening Bulletin,* with the caption: "Chico Ruiz steals home as psy-chic father, wheezing daughter, and Lead Bottom look on." Or better yet: "Aunt Nelle runs onto field and kicks Ma-HEY-fey in the balls."

"That was bad," I muttered.

"Bad," Dad repeated, still staring at home plate.

"How did you know he was going to run?"

"I could feel it."

"Really?"

"I just knew it."

As we sat, I turned to Linda. "What's the 'H' for?"

"What?"

"The guy behind us said, 'Jesus H. Christ.'"

She laughed. "Hector."

"*Hector?*"

She giggled more. I swung around to Dad. "Linda says Jesus' middle name is Hector."

Dad leaned over to her. "That is not funny."

Linda slunk in her seat.

Dad continued. "His middle name was Howard."

Linda burst out laughing. And I was reminded that Dad would do anything for a joke. It included the caveat, "Don't tell your mother any of this."

For the next three innings the crowd was restless as the 1-0 lead held. We sat under a full moon. I wondered how Dad knew about Chico Ruiz. The only one who could know something like that was Lassie. What else could he "see"? Did he know that Frank Zampino was drawing cartoon dicks in homeroom and I was laughing at them?

I thought about Mom, who had waved goodbye hours before: "Make sure they win!" It would be crappy if we lost.

That morning, I had come down early for breakfast. Typically I was a laggard for this meal, knowing that if Mom and Dad had argued the night before, there would be tension aplenty. Since spring, though, their hearts tagged along with the good fortune of the Phils. Once, Mom nodded to a TV shot of our manager, Gene Mauch, and said, "He's a good-looking guy, isn't he?" I expected a jealous silence from Dad that would later erupt into a high-decibel 10-rounder. Instead, he held up his wedding ring and grinned, "Your mother knows a good-looking man when she sees one."

The aroma of scrapple hustled me into the kitchen, where I found a plate of it on the Formica table next to a bottle of Karo syrup. WCAU Radio was on, volume low, and Mom stood at the stove murdering a pan of already-too-brown scrambled eggs.

"Two thousand fans showed up at the airport!" she said excitedly.

"Wow!"

"Everyone says they'll wrap it up by the weekend."

I sat and gulped my juice. Upstairs, I heard one of my sisters enter the bathroom with Diana Ross on full blast: *"But all you do is treat me bad, Break my heart and leave me sad..."* Under the table, our dog, Duchess, waited patiently for the chewy eggs I would invariably offer.

Mom spun around with a smile and a one-candled cupcake. I had forgotten it was September 21.

"Happy Half Birthday!"

It may have been odd to mark such a day, but Mom always did, and I had come to believe it was because my birth—now eleven and a *half* years ago—had been so difficult. On top of the cupcake she had iced the stitches of a baseball and the Phillies "P." I laughed, and my appreciation fueled her with a skip back to the stove.

"I thought since you were going to the game tonight..."

Mom worked the fry pan with the keep-busy intensity that defined her early 40s. Her tight, pretty face, topped by bright auburn hair, seemed just a romantic kiss away from dissolving into the soft, cinematic gorgeousness I had seen in older photos. Still at the stove, her back to me, she said, "Your father loves taking you to these games. You know he never had a father to take him."

I blew out the candle with a confident wish.

The bottom of the ninth opened with a bang as Wes Covington hit one off the scoreboard and slid headfirst into second. We were back in business.

"That's our sixth hit," Linda said.

Adolfo Phillips pinch-ran for Covington, and Dad was into it. "Tying run in scoring position!"

I rifled through my Phillies yearbook to find Phillips. I felt better re-reading that he was a "slender Panamanian speedster." That should be enough to get a run in.

Cincy starter John Tsitouris forced John Herrnstein to pop up. Then he got Clay Dalrymple on a grounder to second, as Phillips moved to third.

Tony Taylor stepped in, scratched the dirt, and made the sign of the cross. I made a split-second decision to cross myself and hoped that no one saw. If it got back to Grams that I had invoked a *Roman* blessing, I could kiss my happy childhood goodbye. In a snap, Taylor was on first with a walk.

The crowd cheered, rose, and cheered louder. Shortstop Ruben Amaro dug in. Strike one only increased our will.

"He's our hottest hitter," I told Linda through the noise.

Strike two did not deter us. Connie Mack was rocking as Amaro had the moment: runners on the corners, two outs and two strikes in the bottom in the ninth. Everyone was standing. I hopped up and down, hollering. The noise was deafening.

Tsitouris delivered.

Amaro took it.

Strike three.

Instant silence.

We seemed frozen, unwilling to process it. Fans picked up their things and began to leave, but Dad took in the field longingly. It seemed forever.

Finally, as we walked up the aisle, I fumbled to fill the silence.

"You know that dance we did when they beat the Giants and moved into first? We're going to do a crazier one after the World Series!"

Dad nodded and half-smiled. His first-place swagger had vanished into the night, but I tried not to read his eyes.

We would win tomorrow.

DAD VS. GRAMS

I first remember reading Dad's eyes five years earlier, when we lived in northern Virginia and my only brush with baseball was a quick study of ball club patches on the wagon-red jacket Mom bought for me at a thrift store.

We had spent the afternoon across the Potomac visiting Grams, who lived with Mom's sister and brother-in-law, Aunt Elsie and Uncle Jimmy. Their place in White House Heights, Maryland, was a creaky wood house besieged by overgrown shrubs and ringed by a shabby picket fence that kept nothing in or out.

I found myself in Grams's room, where a slight breeze from the open window was no relief from the early summer mugginess. Grams sat at her vanity. She massaged her high cheekbones with a fair amount of Pond's Cold Cream and then turned to me as if moving to the next task. Her classic German face, with its steel eyes and stiff mouth, tipped back just enough to regard me as her subject.

"What did you learn in Sunday School this week?

I looked away.

"You must have learned *something*. What miracle did Jesus perform?"

"He dug in the ground till he hit China."

Grams sighed. She nodded to her framed paint-by-number

Jesus to indicate that He—of the number-1 blue eyes, number-3 golden locks, and number-7 flesh hands—was watching. She and Woolworth's Jesus had me. I had to fess up that I was bored by Sunday School and might never be as good a Lutheran as all the Haatvedts, Ingvoldstads, and Didszoneits who populated our church.

"I didn't pay attention."

Grams chuckled with self-satisfaction. While her favorite TV character, Perry Mason, took a full 60 minutes to elicit a sobbing courtroom confession, she had trapped me in 10 seconds with the aid of a $3.95 hobby kit. Years later, when I learned that J. Edgar Hoover had worn a dress, I had to consider that he may have been my grandmother.

Now that it was determined I was going to hell, Grams turned to the next task—sorting dimes. I had done this before, so I knew to hold the Dixie cup just at the lip of the vanity, as Grams separated an ample pile of coins. The Liberty Heads stayed and the FDRs plopped into the cup, which she would return to the bank. I imagined her headstone: "Here lies Grams. She never carried a Roosevelt dime."

As my cup got heavier, her annoyance grew.

"He led us to ruin with his socialism," she proclaimed. "And here it is 1959, and I can't say Eisenhower is much better. Eisenhower wasn't really a Republican, you know. He stole the nomination from Bob Taft, who was a good conservative from a good Republican family. And do you know what the *Democrats* might do next year?"

No idea.

"Put up a *Catholic!*" she continued. She closed her eyes and shivered at the thought of it.

Hardly a day went by when Grams did not scour the papers for proof that the evil papists with their 10-children families were grouping for a final assault against Anglo-Saxon Protestantism. The orders would be whispered Bingo player to Bingo player, the army would be assembled at a Friday night fish fry and—*bam!*—Lutherans would be back in Rome, kissing the hem of John XXIII. Grams, however, would not go down without a fight. Ever since she picked up a rumor that the Catholic Church owned Pillsbury, none of the company's products was allowed in her house.

Dad walked in and rescued me.

"We're feeding Opie," he said.

Grams and Dad locked eyes. You could almost hear the score from *High Noon*. She frowned and turned back to her mirror.

I ran into the dining room, where everyone was gathered around the young opossum Dad had trapped in our garage. Aunt Elsie had placed it in a large wood and wire hutch, where it inched toward a plate of strawberry puree. Aunt Elsie had a plain, friendly face and brownish-blond hair sectioned by barrettes; she spent her days reading dusty novels and completing various arts and crafts, including the paint-by-number projects that hung here and there. Disappointed by childlessness, she became mother to a menagerie of pets. In any corner of the house, you could stumble upon an out-sized box turtle, wounded crow, or some feral hobo.

"Let's take Mutt for a walk," she would say, as she leashed her dog. "He has to do his pop."

When Mutt squatted, she would chuckle. "Oh, here comes his *pop*!"

Her use of this word was instantly disturbing to me. And became even more so when she livened up the reporting.

"Snap ... crackle ...," she would start. "Pop!" she would declare, as his shit hit the ground.

If Mutt were full, she'd have a good laugh every 20 feet.

"Snap ... crackle ... pop!"

"Snap ... crackle ... pop!"

I never ate Rice Krispies again. If a film crew had been around, she would have put Kellogg's out of business.

So dogs did pop. While cats, I learned, were let out to do their "business."

"Where's Snoopy?" I would ask.

"Off doing his business."

Cats, evidently, had turned this pooping thing into a fabulous enterprise. I never saw them do it, and just like that, they were back in the house having done it. But somewhere, I suspected, hush-hush profits were being made.

Opie, whose evacuation habits had not yet been colorfully defined, sniffed the strawberry puree.

Linda got up close to the hutch. "His tail is creepy."

"It's called a prehensile tail," Aunt Elsie said. "He can *hang* from it."

"Make him do it!" I said, as I danced around with a parakeet on my finger.

"Not just yet," Aunt Elsie said.

I lifted the parakeet to face paint-by-number wildcat.

"You'll never believe how I found it," Dad was quick to tell Aunt Elsie. "I was in the dark part of the garage, going through old boxes, and saw a pair of eyes staring back at me. Immediately, I smelled a rat."

My oldest sister, Ginger, got the teen giggles.

Before Dad could launch into his comedy bit, Grams appeared in the living room at her grand piano.

"Who wants to hear Beethoven?" she called out.

Ginger and Linda scrambled to their feet.

"Excuse me, Hal," Aunt Elsie said.

Three bars into "Fur Elise," we were all gathered around the piano, except for Dad, who stood alone in the dining room. I could tell he was really steamed.

Grams swept into Brahms' Capriccio in G minor, and the frisky music seemed an antidote to her hearty harrumphs at the world. It was easy to think she was lost in memory. Back when she studied at the conservatory. Back when she lived in a fine house near Pittsburgh, with the husband she adored, before he died of congestive heart failure when Mom was just nine. She finished with a flourish, and we applauded.

"Your grandfather loved the Fantasias," she smiled. "The Capriccio was his favorite."

"Tell us how he built a car," I said.

"Oh, he could do anything," she laughed. "He read the classics and could talk for hours on any subject. He was a practical man, yet our house had its elegant appointments. He was certainly no *skinflint*."

I cringed. Seconds later, I heard the back screen door slam shut. Paint-by-number Humpty Dumpty nearly fell off the wall.

It was dusk as we drove home through Washington in our Pontiac station wagon, and the setting sun bathed the city's monuments in a warm, pinkish hue. Dad was at the wheel, still stewing over his loss to Grams. Near Third and Independence, Mom pointed to a building.

"That's where your dad and I met. We were both working in the War Department, which had a little drama club. I was making posters for a play, and your dad came up to my apartment to see if I needed help. We ended up in Rock Creek Park on our first date!"

We'd heard the story before. But Mom wasn't telling it for us.

She looked at Dad, coaxing him into the romance. "Remember your old car? The two-seater?"

He kept his eyes on the road. Mom turned, finally, and lost herself out the passenger window.

"Anyway," she said, "that's where we worked. I remember standing there after Pearl Harbor and listening to the president declare war." She paused. "It was all so sad."

After several minutes of driving in a tomb, I piped up.

"Why is Grams upset with Catholics?"

"Because they *cross themselves*," Ginger said. "Plus, Uncle Art [Mom's brother] married a Catholic."

Mom turned around. "Aunt Mary was *not* Catholic. She was Eastern Orthodox."

"Grams still went ape at their wedding," Ginger insisted.

I could see in the rearview mirror that Dad had brightened.

"Part of the service was in Latin," Mom explained. "And when the priest referred to Art as *Arturo*, she got a little upset."

Ginger rolled her eyes. "A little upset? She screamed and fainted! They had to carry her out like a sack of potatoes!"

Dad laughed.

"Linda wants to marry a horse!" I said.

Linda hit me. "Shut up!"

"Grams would faint!" Ginger said.

Mom put her foot down. "You kids be respectful to Grams."

"Yes," Dad said to Linda. "Be respectful to Grams. If you marry a horse, make sure he's a Lutheran."

We laughed, and Dad was beaming again. He had delivered the punch line *and* tweaked his nemesis—all after learning that Linda's wedding might be purchased for a mere bucket of oats.

One little joke had flipped the entire mood. And Mom *could* have continued her story. A year after Pearl Harbor, she and Dad were married. Dad crossed the Atlantic and fought in France and Germany, rising to the rank of army captain. Mom worked in the War Department personnel office, where she claimed to have spurned the untoward advances of many men, including a general. Dad returned with a Bronze Star and stayed in the military, working in the information office of the new Department of Defense. They had survived the horrible convulsions that swallowed so many others and made it to the summit of the American Century, where in 1951, on an annual salary of $6,500, Dad bought a three-bedroom house in Alexandria for $18,000, venetian blinds included.

We sailed down Russell Road, past the Braddock Cannon of the Revolution, past nice homes with neat lawns, and turned left to 30 West Myrtle Street. I hopped out, and the smell of honeysuckle welcomed me. I stood under giant oaks and sycamores, at the front porch of our foursquare American Craftsman home. The moon was already above the eaves of our house as we walked up the steps.

Inside, it was a steam bath, and Dad went about opening windows. Mom took our youngest sister, Susan, up to bed, and the rest of us ran into the living room to watch *Zorro*. Ginger clicked the channel knob on the RCA, a futuristic box propped up by four spindly legs.

It wasn't long before Zorro leaped off a mission roof onto a waiting horse, as the captain's witless soldiers stumbled after him. I loved the show. But one thing always bothered me. Every time the rotund Sergeant Garcia saw the sword mark "Z," he was so amazed. "Zorro!" he would exclaim. Of course it was Zorro! It was Zorro this time, the time before, and the time before that. Why was Sergeant Garcia so surprised? Who else would it be? Had Zsa Zsa Gabor or Zeppo Marx been in town, I could have understood a little startle in his voice. It was all so silly.

Our orange and white kitten, Taffy, scooted across the plain, low-back sofa, as Dad swept through the room turning off every light—

"Who am I—General Electric?"

Zorro was cornered and about to be unmasked, but launched into his nifty gymnastics, outsmarted an army of trained swordsmen and won the day. Mom called us up for our baths. As Ginger and Linda sprinted up the squeaky hardwood stairs, Dad held me back.

"Did you have a good time today?"

I nodded.

He took a nickel out of his pocket and held it out.

"You can have this if you tell me something," he said. "What did Grams say about me?"

I stiffened my back.

"When you were in her room—did she talk about me?"

"No." I shrugged and looked away.

"You're sure?"

"Yes."

It was about this time that I realized our family had issues. Grams was obsessed with Catholics. Dad was obsessed with Grams.

Aunt Elsie delighted in the word "pop." And Linda wanted to marry a horse. As a kid, I didn't know what to make of it. There was no paint-by-number Freud.

Dad gave me the nickel.

"Grams gave me a *dime*," I said.

I had him.

He coughed up another five cents, and I ran upstairs feeling as crafty as Zorro.

BROUHAHA

TEAM	WINS	LOSSES	PCT.	G.B.
National League Standings Morning of September 22, 1964				
Philadelphia	90	61	.596	--
Cincinnati	84	66	.560	5.5
St. Louis	83	66	.557	6
San Francisco	83	68	.550	7
Milwaukee	77	72	.517	12
Pittsburgh	76	72	.514	12.5
Los Angeles	75	75	.500	14.5
Chicago	67	82	.450	22
Houston	64	88	.421	26.5
New York	50	99	.336	39

I do not like onions.

Nor did I like the insidious way Mom dumped them into everything she cooked. So I was chagrined (again) when she opened the stove and lifted out a bubbly-hot cauldron of her Hunter's Stew, a concoction of ground beef, rice, potatoes, tomatoes, and the slimy objects of my disaffection.

I tried to shake it off. "Did Dad tell you about his premonition?"

Mom rolled her eyes. "Only a hundred times."

"I can't believe we lost," I said, collapsing my body into a pouty trudge through the dining room. Mom breezed ahead. She cleared her Goldwater fliers off the well-worn oak table and stacked them on a nearby teacart.

"Well, everybody's gunning for us, so the pitchers need to hold the runners on tight," she said. "The Dodgers stole *six* bases off us on Saturday."

Her white, sleeveless blouse and pale-green skirt formed an hourglass at her trim waist, which seemed the swiveling engine of her energy. She quickly set placemats on the table, and I followed her around with silverware. Dad walked in with the paper.

"No one in his right mind would break for home with Robinson up," he said, sitting and shaking his head. "The guy's lucky he made it, or he'd be packing his bags for the minors."

"Mom says it's the pitcher's fault."

"Pretty much," Dad nodded, as I hopped into my seat. "Generally, you steal off the pitcher, not the catcher. If the runner gets a good enough jump, the best throw in the world won't help. Pitchers need to look the runner back. They need good peripheral vision."

He demonstrated by catching me with the corner of his eye.

"That's why you don't see any nuns pitching in the big leagues," he said. "Too much head gear."

Dad grinned, and I burst out laughing. At the head of the table, when his mood was easygoing, Dad reminded me of a wisecracking TV host. Mom often said he looked like Art Linkletter, and I could see it now as I regarded his high forehead, twinkling eyes, and face flushed with monkey business.

The Hunter's Stew arrived and, on its heels, another horror. Mom set a dish of lima beans only inches from me. I was nearly nauseated.

"Smells good," Dad said.

Just my luck that Mom married another vegetable lover. Had Dad been a man of my tastes, he could have long ago negotiated an end to the torment. We'd be eating stacks of Pez this very instant. I looked across the table at Susan, who seemed delighted by my predicament. Linda bounded in with her radio tuned to WIBG, Philly's rock and roll station that we called "Wibbage." Mom bristled.

"Not at the table," she said.

"It's the Beatles!" Linda huffed, before clicking it off.

"Have they cut their hair yet?" Mom wanted to know.

Linda rolled her eyes. Then Susan did. Then I did. Eye rolling was such a staple of communication at our house that one ridiculous comment could set off a chain reaction that sometimes included the dog.

"If I could sell records like that, I'd wear hair down to my ankles," Dad declared, offering a throaty audition: "She loves you yeah, yeah, yeah! She loves you yeah, yeah, yeah!"

Mom deadpanned. "If your father sees a singing career, I think his ESP is history."

We laughed.

"Do you think we'll bounce back?" I asked the table.

"Well, Short has 17 wins," Dad said. "One more tonight and he'll have a good shot at 20."

He was too matter-of-fact. But added, "World Series tickets went on sale today."

I was stoked! "Really? Can we go?"

Linda brightened.

"Absolutely," Dad smiled. Mom added a happy nod of assent.

"Who are we going to play?" Linda asked.

"Probably the Yankees," Mom figured. "Although it could be the Orioles or White Sox."

"You're *sure* we can get tickets?"

"I'll go see the mayor," Dad replied.

And that, I was sure, sealed the deal. Mayor William G. Rohrer, Jr. was the imposing local legend that ruled the altar upon which our family's most lofty requests were placed. Dad banked at his bank and bought our cars from Rohrer Chevrolet. In return, my sisters and I got summer jobs at the bank and New Jersey state scholarships for college. Mom also worked for a while in the personnel department.

Mayor Rohrer eschewed an inner-sanctum office at Peoples National Bank. Instead, he sat at a desk in the lobby, where he could spy on the coming and going of loyalists as he lunched with great relish on sloppy hoagies and Dunkin' Donuts. When visiting the bank, Dad would conduct his business and then stand suppliantly until the mayor motioned him over. Dad would light up and sidle to the desk, where favors would be asked and often granted.

On election day, Dad rode around town with a huge man named Dolph Siegel to get out the vote. When I was in high school, all of this "innocent back scratching," as Dad called it, did not approach the teenage cachet wielded by my classmate, Bob Love, whose Uncle Adamucci was rubbed out during a suspected mob hit at the Rickshaw Inn in Cherry Hill, but it was my personal introduction to Civics 101, and I loved it.

Confident that a World Series—*a freakin' World Series!*—was a turnstile-click away, I got back to managing the meal. With surgical precision, I separated the tiny onion bits from the stew and moved them to the side of the plate, where a large potato slice quickly concealed them. This was accomplished with master stealth, to avoid detection by the vegetable overlords or my siblings, who would surely rat me out for a sack of pennies.

My ally, Duchess, took up position under the table. She was our cute pound pup—part collie, part cocker spaniel and soon to be part lima bean.

The lima bean drop was accomplished with equal cunning. I moved each bean with my left pinkie to the edge of the plate, and then, in one fluid motion, cupped it in my hand. In a nanosecond, my hand was under the table and the bean was released—to fall soundlessly on our brown, wall-to-wall carpet and be gobbled up by Duchess. Sometimes, during the left-hand drop, I would raise a glass of milk with my right hand to divert attention, and if too much suspicion fell on my left hand, I would accomplish the drop with my right.

A million magicians practicing a million sleights of hand for a million years could not approach my genius.

"Stop feeding Duchess!" Mom said. "And eat your onions!"

"They're under his potato!" Susan shouted gleefully.

Mom sighed. "How do you expect to grow up to be healthy if you don't eat your vegetables?"

"Lead Bottom," Susan whispered in my direction.

I was hopelessly caught. And learned that Mom had a better pick-off move than our pitchers. But that wasn't the end of it. She went into the kitchen and returned with my *Boy Scout Handbook*. The one with the smiling Norman Rockwell scout on the cover. The one whose introduction insisted, "You are the American on whom the future of our wonderful country depends."

She sat and leafed through it. "We'll see about your bad habits."

Lightning iced my veins. This was it. My *mother* was turning to page 425—the page that had been dog-eared at summer camp and read by flashlight by the half-dozen howling scouts who packed into my tent. A rush of fear locked my brain.

"From boy to man," Mom recited.

Susan's jaw dropped.

"These changes are caused by the function of the sex glands or testicles," Mom continued.

Linda cranked up Wibbage and held it to her ear.

"At times, the glands discharge part of their secretions through the sex organ during sleep," she plowed on. *"This process is called a nocturnal emission, or 'wet dream.'"*

Dad stared ahead, his fork full of Hunter's Stew frozen in mid-air.

"There are boys who do not let nature have its own way with them, but cause the emissions themselves," she declared with stern emphasis.

Duchess rolled her eyes.

I wiped my clammy face with a napkin and finally came to.

"Here it is," Mom said. "Page 275."

I blinked. My brain unlocked.

"In planning tasty meals for camp," she read, *"it is important to include all the foodstuffs you need for good health. These include potatoes, beets, cauliflower, onions."*

"Why are you sweating?" Linda demanded.

"Because he doesn't eat his vegetables," Susan laughed.

How pathetic that my only solace was that Mom had *not* used the word "testicles" at dinner. If the future of America depended on my character and my character depended on the eating of onions, then "our wonderful country" was in for a bumpy ride. Why couldn't the Boy Scouts ditch their dietary jingoism, stick to teaching knots, and leave me alone?

Dinner was a distant memory when we settled into the living room to hear By Saam, Bill Campbell, and Richie Ashburn call the game on WFIL, AM 560. A fine breeze found us through the open panes of our bay window. The main pieces in this room were an apricot velvet sofa, Dad's olive-leather recliner, paisley occasional chair, and the off-white credenza packed with Mom's records. Mom decided that this fine mishmash should be tied together with Chinese accents that included two pairs of bronze symbols, which Mom and Dad often discussed.

"These two mean peace."

"No. Those are happiness. *These* are peace."

"The lady at the store said they were peace."

"She said they were happiness."

"That old woman wouldn't know happiness if she saw it."

"I'm telling you, *that's* happiness and *this* is peace!"

"You're wrong! If we had a Chinese person here, he'd tell you!"

"Where are we going to find a *Chinese person* at this hour?"

As the pre-game show ended, Dad nested in his recliner, sans suit jacket and shoes, and picked through the paper. He always read the sports page before dinner and, afterward, concentrated on politics and the comics, which Mom claimed were one and the same. Mom and I sat at either end of the sofa, while Duchess reposed at Mom's feet, ready to receive love pats when the Phils scored.

I felt confident when the lineups were announced, since all of my favorite Phillies were starting. Leading off was Cookie Rojas, our versatile spark plug, who had already played *seven* positions during 1964. Our double-play combination of Bobby Wine and Cookie was affectionately dubbed, "The Days of Wine and Rojas." Batting third was sweet-swinging rightfielder Johnny Callison, the sure-to-be National League MVP. At cleanup was third baseman Richie Allen, our rookie slugger on the brink of a 30-homer, 200-hit season. And on the mound was Chris Short, the team's ERA leader and, according to Dad, the best thing from Delaware since cheap gasoline.

My confidence took a beating right off, as Short was not crisp. In the top of the third, he even walked the Reds pitcher, Jim O'Toole.

"Mickey Vernon used to fine his guys 50 bucks if they walked the opposing pitcher," Dad said of the former Washington Senators skipper.

"Some managers use fines, some throw ribs," Mom smiled, referring to Gene Mauch's infamous tantrum late in the '63 season, when he trashed a locker room buffet and splattered his players with barbecue sauce.

Mauch, who at 38 was the youngest manager in the majors, did have a combative style, but he had transformed the woeful Phillies into a contender with his intense gamesmanship, opportune use of the hit-and-run, and smart platoon system: Ruben Amaro and Bobby Wine at shortstop, Clay Dalrymple and Gus Triandos behind the plate.

After a single, another walk, and a force, O'Toole scored. It was 1-0 Reds, with Pete Rose on third, Vada Pinson on first and Frank Robinson at bat. In another bit of Reds daring, Pinson broke for second on a delayed steal. Triandos threw the ball into center field, and Rose scored, making it 2-0.

"What is it with them stealing when Robinson is up?" I asked.

Dad was irked. "That's a big 'E' on Triandos. And that's why I said *generally* you steal off the pitcher. Here's a case where it's the catcher's fault. At least first base is open, so they can walk Robinson."

When Mauch decided to pitch to Robinson, Dad moved from "irked" to "riled," which meant shouting at inanimate objects such as the radio.

"What are you doing?" he screamed, losing control of essential facial muscles. "The guy has 27 homers!"

When Robinson connected on a full-count slider for number 28, and a 4-0 Reds lead, Dad moved from "riled" to "pissed." He got up and paced like a zoo panther.

"Nobody listens to me!"

Mom sighed and shut her *Better Homes & Gardens*, and I started to think Linda and Susan had the right idea down in the family room, watching the premiere of *The Man From U.N.C.L.E.* The phone rang, and Mom indicated that I should get it. If Dad answered, it could be someone else who wouldn't listen to him. I ran into the kitchen.

"Hello?"

"So, what do you think of Mauch's dumb managing? Now we're in a pickle, and if we lose tonight, we'll be only four and a half games to the good."

Aunt Nelle's questions were not to be answered; they were inserted merely to add a bouncy rhythm to her septuagenarian monologues. I grinned, figuring I was also about to hear her most recent maligning moniker. For most of the season, Gus Triandos was known as "Big Leather," recalling his days with the Orioles, when he wore an enormous glove to catch the knuckleballer Hoyt Wilhelm. But when Aunt Nelle noticed him continually fidgeting with his chest protector, a juicier jibe was born.

"What's wrong with this bunch?" she went on. "Last night Ma-HEY-fey throws it away, and now Fussy Gussy chucks one into center field."

I laughed.

"I might have to go down to the stadium and bawl them out!"

"Last night we almost won it in the ninth," I said.

"Almost? What kind of rally does Mauch expect when he trots out that Pop-up King Herrnstein? I hear you're coming to visit your old great aunts on Sunday."

"We are!"

"Well, maybe the Phils will have righted things by then and we can celebrate a pennant. I have a bottle of hooch under the sink, and we can throw back a few belts. Then you can show me all your speedy moves from Little League."

I froze. *Was she kidding? Who told her?* I panicked and handed the phone to Dad, who was itching for a bitch fest. He started right in: "Why do we pitch to their best hitter with Short struggling and first base open?"

I sat back on the sofa.

"Aunt Nelle says we're going to get sauced on her 'hooch' when the Phillies clinch it."

Mom laughed. "She's something, isn't she?"

"A riot."

"When I was a girl, she'd take me to Forbes Field on 10-cent Ladies Days. We'd sit in the bleachers and have a ball. Of course, Mother didn't like it. She didn't approve of baseball." Mom shook her head. "You never saw two sisters more different than Grams and Aunt Nelle."

"Grams is not really a riot."

"Well, it was tough for her after Daddy died. She took a lot of odd jobs and held onto the house for as long as she could. Things would have been so different if Daddy had lived," she said gently. "I would have gone to art school or college."

In the sixth, Richie Allen made a throwing error and Fussy Gussy had *two* passed balls. "The boo-birds are out tonight," By Saam reported, as we heard a cascade of catcalls.

"Philly fans would boo a one-legged grandmother," Dad said.

I pictured Grams hopping about the infield as an angry mob pelted her with Roosevelt dimes.

In the top of the eighth, our reliever, Ed Roebuck, plunked Chico Ruiz in apparent retaliation for his steal of home the night before. Ruiz then swiped second base. Between innings, with the Reds thrashing us 9-1, Ruiz jogged out to play third. A ball flew out of the Phillies dugout and just missed his head, causing both benches to empty in what By Saam often called "an old-fashioned brouhaha."

"This is ridiculous," Mom said. "They're acting like a bunch of thugs."

"Sometimes a fight is a *good* thing," Dad countered. "It fires up the troops."

"What if they get hurt?"

"No one's going to get hurt."

"What if they lose someone for the World Series?"

"I'm telling you—no one's going to get hurt."

"They're throwing punches!"

"Nobody ever lands a punch in one of these things. They just roll around on the ground."

"Says who?"

"Says me." Dad raised his voice. "So don't tell me I don't know what a fight is."

Trouble. If Mom raised her voice in return, it could be a long night. I shut my eyes. *Please, God, don't let them fight. Just make them yell at me, not at each other.*

I heard a wheezy cough. I opened my eyes and looked at Duchess. The cough turned into a hack, and the hack turned into gulping convulsions. She gave it one last heave and spit up a green, soupy vomit filled with tiny chunks of lima beans.

Mom looked at the mess in horror and then fixed her anger on me. Prayers, I discovered, are occasionally answered.

I ran for the hills.

LUTHERAN SHTICK

There's nothing like believing you're about to die. Especially if you have to give up bunk beds and a cool bike.

It was the fall of 1962. I was on the upper playground at Maury School in Alexandria and transfixed by the distant sky, where, every few seconds, another plane would sail by on its approach to Washington National. These were military planes, I thought, on the way to bomb Cuba. When they did, Cuban missiles would be fired at us. I walked out past the monkey bars and turned away so no one would see me crying. I wondered if it would hurt to be "evaporated."

In school, we did duck-and-cover drills and were told to act like a turtle if the bomb went off. But everything I picked up from adult whispers or the tense men on TV told me it was all or nothing. My hometown would still be my hometown. Or it would be a puddle of turtle soup.

And I loved my hometown.

Two years before, we had moved several blocks from Myrtle Street to 202 West Glendale Avenue. It was a Georgian colonial, modest in size, with a half-round portico. The master bedroom was on the first floor, and off the dining room was a screened porch that overlooked a sloping back yard lined with poplars. The basement had a finished rec room with Dutch doors, where we could bang on the piano to our hearts' content. Upstairs, Linda and Susan shared a bedroom, while Ginger and I got our own. Mine, sporting brand-new bunk beds, was painted pale yellow.

So when I heard the crisis was over and saw a hundred looks of relief, I leaped onto my emerald American Flyer and rode with abandon down every block from Russell Road to Commonwealth Avenue and Braddock Boulevard to King Street. I was just happy to roll over leaves and acorns and feel the sweet air in my face.

Grams, of course, blamed the whole ordeal on President Kennedy, and somehow managed to indict his Catholic aides, Catholic brother, and Catholic, rum-running father. Jackie was cleared of the affair, but drew a sharp rebuke for doing The Twist.

At church and elsewhere, though, the president was a hero. As Aunt Nelle put it the following Thanksgiving, "Jack really put one over on that cue ball head Khrushchev."

Mom was a Republican, but more moderate than Grams. By moderate, I mean that while she disliked Roosevelt's policies, she still carried all manner of coins in her purse. I got the feeling Dad was a Republican just to win the approval of Mom's family, which, next to saving three cents apiece by ordering us hamburgers instead of cheeseburgers at the Hot Shoppe, seemed at the top of his to-do list.

In 1960, Mom and Dad were for Nixon, and Mom kept the "Nixon-Lodge" sticker on our front-door window for years after the election. I watched a few minutes of one of the presidential debates and remember thinking only that Kennedy had a big head and Nixon looked like a bank robber.

The stuff of substance I noted came from our new pastor, Carl Beyer. The previous minister, H.J. Wuebbens, was an exhausting grouch, and I had little time for his barbarous Old Testament characters. If Nebuchadnezzar had been as affable as Buffalo Bob, things would have turned out a lot better for everybody. Pastor Beyer was a jovial man who honked rather than laughed and made his points with pipe in hand, which highlighted both his intellect and casual manner. His sermons were about real people in Alexandria, and it was the first time I was captivated on Sundays.

To the grumblings of some in our all-white church, Pastor Beyer preached for civil rights and supported Martin Luther King Jr.'s March on Washington. Mom and Dad seemed supportive.

"When I was in school," Mom said, "a young black girl joined our class. At recess, I was the only one who would hold her hand."

Dad said simply, "Good and bad people come in all colors."

The only African American I really knew was a woman named Pecola. When we lived on Myrtle Street, she would come on Fridays to take care of us while Mom ran errands. She was fun, and I was her favorite. Dad drove her home at dusk, and when I rode along, we had a lot of laughs along the way. She lived in a small, square house made of brick or cinder block in what some people called the "rough" section of Alexandria. Dad always got out, opened the car door, and walked her to the house.

Mom and Dad treated Pecola with respect, and in matters of race and dignity, that's all I knew about my parents.

If they had been as nice to each other, life would have been idyllic. But they fought. Dad could take a syllable the wrong way and blow up. Mom, his equal in smarts and verve, would either soothe his hurt or simply not tolerate it. They clashed about money and things to be done around the house, about why we were lost driving and why we were driving in the first place. One thing was certain: In the early '60s, my sisters and I heard more arguments than the Warren Court.

The little spats could be downright hilarious. Like the time Dad won the grand prize at our school raffle.

"A giant stuffed panda!" he exclaimed.

"The kids will love it!" Mom replied. "They have stuffed bears, but no stuffed giant panda."

"What do you mean 'stuffed giant panda'? It's a *giant* stuffed panda. Look at the size of it."

"No. Actually, it *is* a stuffed giant panda. A giant panda is a kind of panda."

"Oh, come on. When people think of a panda, they think of this kind. It's a giant stuffed panda."

"Stuffed giant panda."

"Giant stuffed panda."

"No!"

"All right. Let's call it a giant stuffed giant panda."

"Fine."

"I don't see why you had to make a whole big thing out of it."

"I *didn't* make a big whole thing out of it. You did."

"Did you say 'big whole thing'?"

The real fights, however, were no laughing matter. My sisters and I braved repeated episodes of shouting and door slamming. Once, a plate was smashed. The word "divorce" hovered about, but nothing came of it.

Soon, a sort of domestic evolution began to shape our sibling brains. All kids hunger for attention. But in our case, attention came with a huge dividend: The more Mom and Dad were focused on us, the less they would quarrel with each other. Ginger and Linda, perhaps unconsciously, had already carved out their strategies.

Ginger, freckle-faced and brimming with creativity, became the achiever. Her art show paintings were featured in the paper, and her Halloween costumes, including a devil whose tail trailed for half a block, were the stuff of neighborhood legend. She would graduate from George Washington High School first in her class.

I learned the hard way that sibling talents were not necessarily transferable. Ginger played viola in the high school orchestra and told me that oboe players were most in demand. I became oboe-obsessed until Mom and Dad agreed to rent one and send me to summer music school.

The instructor was a thin, nervous man with the temperament

of a puppy kicker. If a sour note were heard, he would shake his baton and scream for us to stop, clearly annoyed that the parents of northern Virginia had not sent him a candy box of Jascha Heifetzes.

I, for one, played no sour notes. I played no notes at all. Despite several tutorials from the bony despot, I could get *no sound* out of that damn oboe. Its double-cane reed tasted yummy, though, so I nipped at it. Then I began chewing it outright. Dad was irked that he had to buy a *second* reed, and during a family conference I pledged to buckle down and become a serious music student. At the next class, I carefully attached the expensive mouthpiece, placed it gently on my lips and took a deep breath.

I went after it like a beaver.

Having finished my own reed, I salivated for any nearby wood, including some tasty-looking maracas. Horrified, the teacher hauled in my folks.

"Look at this!" he cried, waggling the stumpy reed under their noses. "He has no aptitude. No aptitude at all!"

Dad got a refund from the school, we sent back the oboe, and I spent the rest of the summer gnawing on Popsicle sticks.

Linda was a brilliant student, and I looked up to her, too. But she became the sickly child. She got shots from an allergist who made house calls and arrived with a black bag full of needles. That must be a happy job, I thought: going door-to-door jabbing people. If I had known the address of that jackass from music school, I would've slipped it into the doctor's pocket.

Over time, an adjective popped up and cleaved onto Linda's name. "Leave poor Linda alone," Mom would tell us. "How's poor Linda?" people would ask. Linda became so poor, I expected the Peace Corps to show up any minute.

My one opportunity to win attention as "poor Carl" was a major bust. I was sent home from school with a note that I had "fifth disease." For a week, I endured not only blotchy skin, but the snickers and scorn that accompany such a lamely named ailment. After measles, scarlet fever, German measles, and atypical scarlet fever, doctors had evidently tired of their attempts to color the lexicon, tossing me and my mottled ilk to the mercy of hecklers.

"The blind man came to Jesus and said, 'Jesus, I am without eyes,' and Jesus laid his hand upon the man, and the man cried, 'I can see!' The leper crawled to Jesus and said, 'I am mangled, Lord,' and Jesus touched him, and soon he wept at the fullness of his own body. And the third man came to Jesus and said, 'Jesus, I have disease number thirty-six,' and Jesus laughed and the crowd laughed, and Jesus said, 'Away with you, silly man,' and another man yelled that he should come back four times claiming to have disease number nine, and the crowd laughed once more and put the man on an ass and rode him through the town to be mocked by the suitably sick and appropriately ill."

On the fourth day of fifth disease, I locked myself in my room.

My place in the family order had its roots on a Sunday when friends from church showed up at our house for a potluck supper.

The first to arrive was Hirschie Johnson, a gregarious, back-slapping Texan, whom Dad called "a real operator."

"He waits two or three hours in the Capitol, just to corner a congressman," Dad said. "He knows how to play the game."

"What game?"

"Politics," Dad answered.

"How do you play it?"

"Well, say somebody like Hirschie wants a job or more money for his kid's school. He finds his congressman and turns on the charm."

"Charm?"

"Sure. He tells Congressman Broyhill, 'Hey, I love your suit!' or 'You're doing great things for Alexandria!' And then he'll ask Broyhill to recommend him for some job."

"And he gets it?"

"Oh, sure."

Pastor Beyer and his wife, Herta, walked in from down the street, followed by half the Scandinavian phone book. Among them was Dr. Rolfe Haatvedt, a big, ruddy-faced man with a tremendous shock of snow-white hair. He was abundantly joyful, with a zesty inner compass that always seemed to point him in the direction of fun. Mom could make me laugh with a turn of the phrase. Dad could tell a joke with spot-on delivery. Dr. Haatvedt could *work a room*.

He pushed through the crowd to the Protestant potluck and began lustily. "Smelt casserole! And green lamb!" he roared. "After this, Martin Luther was *begging* for the Diet of Worms!"

There was instant laughter, and the room was ignited.

"Poor Luther. All he could say was, 'Here I stand. I cannot do otherwise. I've had flatulence for months!'"

The room was his. Pastor Beyer spit out his lemonade, and bodies shook so hard I could hear a few other squirts. So great was Dr. Haatvedt's genius, he could use the word "flatulence" and actually produce it in his audience. *Before* dinner, no less.

"You hate our cooking?" a woman called out.

"Yes!" he shouted, to more laughs. "You women get out of the kitchen and start running the country. I'm for Margaret Chase Smith for president!"

There was a smattering of applause.

"Yesterday, a reporter asked, 'Senator Smith, what would you do if you woke up and found yourself in the White House?' She said, 'I would get dressed, run downstairs, apologize to Mrs. Kennedy and leave!'"

Helen Johnson joined in the guffaws, as I pinned her against a bookshelf.

"Your dress is pretty."

"Thank you, dear."

"And you are doing great things for Alexandria."

"Well, thank you."

"Can you tell my parents to buy ice cream instead of ice milk? I hate ice milk."

"What?'

"Your dress is pretty. Please tell my parents to buy ice cream."

Dr. Haatvedt took two giant steps toward me.

"Ice cream? Who needs ice cream when you can have Glug?"

I bit my lip. "Glug?"

He took a sip from his glass and leaned down into my face.

"You don't know about Glug? You don't know about the Glug Maker?"

"No."

The crowd gasped.

"Well, he was the most important man in Norway. For he alone knew how to make the Glug."

Dr. Haatvedt took a swig of his murky punch and smacked his lips. I was drawn in.

"The captain of the greatest ship called his men to attention and announced that the Glug Maker had arrived! A huge barrel for the Glug sat on deck, with the men ringed around it. Soon, the Glug Maker marched aboard, and a cheer went up from stem to stern—Glug! Glug! Glug! Glug!"

Pastor Beyer picked up the chant, and everyone raised a glass: "Glug! Glug! Glug! Glug!"

They hushed.

"The Glug Maker went to work. He walked to the barrel and added water and octopus and blob fish. He tossed in the eyes of a sea snake and the maggoty leg of a Barbary pirate!"

Dr. Haatvedt swallowed his drink. I cringed.

"'Close it!' the Glug Maker ordered. And the men lifted a huge lid onto the barrel and nailed it in place. The sailors danced about, ready for their Glug!"

Dad led another round: "Glug! Glug! Glug! Glug!"

"The barrel was attached to a hoist and lifted high into the air and over the side of the ship. *This* was the moment."

Another hush fell over the room.

"The Glug Maker raised his arm high and brought it down. The rope was cut. The barrel fell. It hit the water and went—"

He paused for effect.

"GLUG."

I blinked several times. And then realized I had been had.

My mouth dropped, and the room exploded in laughter. Dr. Haatvedt tousled my hair and roared. Hirschie Johnson slapped my back: "Got you there, didn't he?"

I broke into a smile, and a little cheer went up.

Later, I would think about how Dr. Haatvedt carved a stage out of the room and how he fooled me with a silly play on words. But for the moment, I had never heard so many people laughing in my house, and I was intoxicated to be in the middle of it.

TOAST OF THE TABLE

National League Standings Morning of September 23, 1964				
TEAM	**WINS**	**LOSSES**	**PCT.**	**G.B.**
Philadelphia	90	62	.592	--
Cincinnati	85	66	.563	4.5
St. Louis	84	66	.560	5
San Francisco	84	68	.553	6
Milwaukee	78	72	.520	11
Pittsburgh	76	73	.510	12.5
Los Angeles	75	76	.497	14.5
Chicago	68	82	.453	21
Houston	64	89	.418	26.5
New York	50	100	.333	39

Dad got big laughs as we gathered in the living room for the 8 o'clock game. He read from the paper: "The Phillies not only have their fans jittery…" He held out his steady hand. "Do I look jittery?"

"No!" we yelled.

"…but have Big Magic, the Honeywell 1400 computer, wavering slightly. Just nine days ago, Big Magic gave the Phillies a 92.4 percent chance of winning their first National League pennant since 1950. Tests conducted this morning in the Computing Center of the Franklin Institute had the Phils rated at 82.3 percent."

He stood there as if addressing his company in WW2.

"Eighty-two percent sounds like a good bet to me. So let's hear it. Are you jittery?"

Mom, Linda, and I held out calm hands and laughed. "No!"

I could tell Dad was covering his worry, but I didn't care. Dinner had been deliciously onion-less, and Mom had topped it off with the crown jewel of her desserts. While her cooking frequently gave me fits, her baking was another matter. The chocolate-chip cookies, brownies, and banana pudding were tops, but it was her pecan pie, which she learned to bake in Mississippi when Dad was stationed north of Jackson, that could make grown men cry and rancid pirates beg for their mamas. I had wheedled a second, substantial slice and was bouncing about in sugar heaven. I was high on pie.

I hopped over to Mom with the front page of the *Evening Bulletin*. "Did you see the World Series tickets?"

"Yes. They're in different colors with the skyline as the backdrop. Very classy."

"Orange is the best color," Dad said. "That's for the deluxe boxes that go for $12 a pop."

"I wish they had turquoise," Mom said.

"You can sit in the blue section for half the game, then switch to the green section," Dad joshed.

"Are you sure we can get some?" I asked, twirling about. "The paper says you have to mail in an application."

"Bring me the paper," Dad said. He read: "There will be 33,608 tickets sold for each game, but about 13,000 are being reserved for season ticket holders and others."

I leaped up. "Yes!"

"Sit down," Mom said. "What's wrong with you?"

"*Big Magic* couldn't figure that out," Linda wisecracked.

"It's those two desserts," Mom deduced.

"You should suck a bag of sugar before Little League," Linda said. "Then they wouldn't call you Lead Butt."

"It's Lead *Bottom!*" I snapped, forced into self-ridicule.

Dad peered over the top of the comics. "He has plenty of energy. He just can't run."

I taunted Linda back. "I should take running lessons from your nose!"

"Leave your sister alone," Mom said, as Linda stuck her nose in an algebra book. "She has health problems."

"Hi, everybody!" greeted us from the radio.

If there was one special voice that floated through our house that year, it belonged to the mellifluous play-by-play legend that had broadcast Philadelphia baseball for 27 years. Byrum "By" Saam Jr. captured the thrills with a steady voice that honored the game with a gentlemanly respect. He also maintained a courtly regard for his booth mates, Campbell and Ashburn: "Thanks so much, Bill!" "Right you are, Rich!"

By never missed an opportunity to promote the team: "Sky-high pop-up, foul, near the third-base seats. Amaro races all the way over from short. He's going to hit the fence on a dead run! He makes the catch! He tumbles over the railing and into the seats, where you and your family can enjoy a great Phils game by calling the ticket office at…" Amaro could have a broken clavicle, a fan could be mangled, but first, by God, By would sell some seats. His malapropisms were legendary, once offering, "And now for all you guys scoring in bed…"

He shared duties with play-by-play pro, Bill Campbell. Campbell's dulcet voice was deeper than Saam's, and he was grounded by a wider knowledge of sports, having routinely broadcast NFL and NBA games. He called perhaps the most famous basketball game of all time, Wilt Chamberlain's 100-point showpiece in 1962 for the Philadelphia Warriors.

Richie Ashburn's second season as a color man was a work in

progress, filled with frequent gaffes, but also insights from his magnificent playing career with the Phillies and hilarious tales from his time with the 1962 Miserable Mets. "I was voted the most valuable player on the worst team in major league history," he said. "There are a lot of ways you can take that!"

I immediately took to the whole broadcasting crew, but Saam was my favorite. Secretly, in my room, I was busy perfecting an impression of him, with all his inflections and pet phrases.

Mauch scowls at umpire Al Barlick, and here he comes out of the dugout. Get ready for a rhubarb!

It's gone! Richie Allen with another tape-measure job to the upper deck!

My repertoire of voices grew to include news anchor Walter Cronkite and various TV characters, including the full cast of *The Beverly Hillbillies*. Lacking an audience, I gathered my monster models, playing to a literal rogues' gallery. It was a tough crowd. The Wolf Man's fangs fell out during my Jack Benny bit, but that had more to do with bad glue than sour punchlines.

Things were peachy as the Phillies took a 1-0 lead into the fourth. But, just like that, Chico Ruiz homered to tie the game.

"That guy is killing us!" Dad groused.

In the sixth, Vada Pinson led off with a drive over the right field wall to put the Reds up 2-1.

"*That* guy is killing us!" Dad heaved.

Mom was resigned. "Maybe they're determined to win it for [former manager] Fred Hutchinson. He has cancer, you know."

"After Gehrig left, the Yankees won the Series," Dad said. "I think he died two years later."

"I remember Gehrig's speech," Mom said. "That was the same year Bob Feller brought his mother to see him pitch. A batter lined one of his fastballs into the stands. It hit his mother and knocked her unconscious."

My parents had moved from cancer to horrible death to

mommy whacking. Nothing like celebrating The Game. I was ready for more pie.

In the bottom of the sixth, with a man on, Alex Johnson came to the plate. Johnson was our speedy rookie outfielder who had played in about 40 games. If there were any questions about his power, he answered them with a 430-foot shot that hit the left field roof. Yes! The Phillies were showing pluck, and it was good to have the lead back, 3-2.

Three singles by Doc Edwards, Leo Cardenas, and Pete Rose in the top of the seventh tied the game 3-3. Then with two on, the home run derby continued as Pinson launched his second of the game over the right field wall. It was 6-3 Reds, but we kept the faith. With balls flying out of the park, anything was possible.

Our opportunity came quickly. The Reds switched pitchers in the bottom of the seventh, bringing in 23-year-old Sammy Ellis. After retiring the first batter, Ellis walked Clay Dalrymple and John Briggs, as the crowd roared.

"The kid is rattled," Dad said.

And so he was. He gave up a third straight walk to Wes Covington.

"One swing for the lead!" I shouted

That's exactly what 23,000 fans were thinking as we heard them rock the stadium. Our clutch hitter, Johnny Callison, was headed to the plate to face the shook-up kid. If we could depend on anyone, it was the gritty Callison. Ten days before, he beat the Giants with a single in the 10th inning. The next day, he hit a two-run homer to lift the Phillies over the Colt .45s. The following day, he singled home the only run of the game.

According to Mom, there were two Phils who could do no wrong: manager Gene Mauch and the wholesome team leader, John Wesley Callison. Callison had grown up dirt poor in Oklahoma, the son of migrant workers. His dogged determination to master every facet of the game won him the attention of the White Sox in 1957, and by the next year he was tearing it up with their Triple-A squad in Indianapolis. In December 1959, the Sox traded him to the Phillies where he soon hit for power (he led the National League in triples in 1962 as an All-Star), stole enough bases to keep opposing pitchers off guard, and ruled right field with a deadly accurate arm. Mom swooned over the most handsome men, and Callison's classic face, with a touch of Cherokee, did not escape her eye. When Callison excelled, Mom glowed like a dreamy debutante. It was the same look she got when she unboxed the latest Tony Bennett album from the Columbia Record Club.

The tension mounted as Ellis worked the count full. The crowd chanted in a raucous bid to unnerve him.

Mom wished out loud. "Come on. Grand slam."

Our doorbell rang.

"Go away!" Dad hollered. "Nobody's home!"

Ellis threw a tough slider. Callison held his swing. It caught the outside corner for strike three.

I pounded the carpet. Dad threw up his hands. And Mom fell back into the couch, 43 again.

"All right," Linda clapped. "A single still scores two."

Tony Taylor, a tough contact hitter, was up. He worked the count to 2-2, but Ellis delivered another perfect slider and caught him looking. The Phils left the bases loaded on two called third strikes and left us speechless.

In the eighth, Richie Allen doubled and scored on a single by Alex Johnson, but that was it. The Reds won 6-4. With the series sweep, they cut our lead to 3 1/2 games, and you could hear Big Magic whirring its calculation of less happy odds.

We sat for a while like a set of flat tires until Linda left for her room.

"That *steal of home* on Monday..." Dad muttered.

"The Reds got lucky," I said. "We're still in first place."

There was another suffocating silence. I glanced at the credenza and thought about playing a comedy album. I wanted to hear the Smothers Brothers and their mischievous moment when "Black is the color of my true love's hair" became "Black is the color of my love's *true* hair." They switched "true" and "love," just as Dr. Haatvedt had fooled me by switching "glug" from a noun to a verb. And we sure needed some laughs.

A minute later, I decided to give it a shot on my own. I stepped up and offered my best Ed Sullivan.

"Tonight, ladies and gentlemen, please welcome…" I twisted for effect. "Please welcome the 1964 World Champion Philadelphia Phillies!"

Dad stared at me. Mom twitched as if a beatnik had broken into the house and "put marijuana" in my Chef Boyardee. I squeezed my face and tried harder.

"Unfortunately, Topo Gigio, the Italian mouse, will not perform tonight, since he was just eaten by an Italian cat."

Nothing.

"I'm pretending to be Ed Sullivan!"

Mom smiled—sort of. "That's cute, honey. Now get down off the coffee table!"

Was that the end of it? What a fine epitaph: "Not even his parents laughed."

Somehow I mined enough moxie to stay in character. I became Ed Sullivan trying to step off the table—twisting about, clumsily akimbo, desperately working to untangle his uncooperative "really big shoes." Mom and Dad chuckled.

"Not bad," Dad said.

Mom laughed harder.

I jumped down and kept it going.

"Ed Sullivan as an umpire!" I imitated Sullivan struggling to call runners "safe" or "out" with his hands glued to his hips. More laughs, and I was sky-high.

Who needed pie?

1963

I began 1963 staring at one of the two most famous women in the world. I ended the year staring at the other.

It was a nippy day in Washington, and the line was long. There were thousands of people who had come to see her. I was with Ginger and Ruth, Dr. Haatvedt's daughter.

"Excited?" Ruth asked me.

"Yep," I replied. "Do you think she'll smile at me?"

"Only if she likes you," Ginger laughed.

I hopped up and down and watched my breath in the cold air. Over the years, I had seen the Declaration of Independence and the "Spirit of St. Louis" and walked to the top of the Washington Monument, counting every step as I went. But this was going to be special. I had seen her on TV and *everywhere*, but I wondered what she looked like up close.

"GW 13, Hammond 0!" I needled Ruth, as we inched along.

"There's always next year," she exhaled.

Ginger and Ruth, who knew each other from church, went to different high schools in Alexandria. The GW-Hammond football game, the battle for the "Bell of Supremacy," was a principal fall affair, and the first sporting event I got to attend. Whoever won the game would paint the Braddock Cannon their colors. Then the city would come out and paint it black again. There was talk of guarding the ancient gun, but the police probably had better things to do than intercept a gaggle of teens in saddle oxfords.

"Ready?" Ginger said, as we entered the building.

I nodded, and we moved along, almost in reverence. In a few minutes, I spotted her, reposed on red velvet with U.S. Marines on either side.

"Wow," I whispered.

I couldn't believe I was in the National Gallery of Art, smiling at the smile of Mona Lisa.

By spring, smiles were hard to come by in our house. Dad's civil service job was eliminated, and things were on edge big time, which meant more quarrels between Mom and Dad. In August, he took a job with Fortress Press, the Lutheran publishing house, and I was happy. Until I heard the word "Philadelphia."

Dad had grown up in South Philly, so the move was a natural for him. I wanted to stay right where I was in Alexandria.

Dad touted "Philly cheese steaks," but I had never heard of a steak in a bun. Mom told me about Pennsylvania Dutch country, but I quickly learned the people were German, not Dutch. Ginger bragged about the Philadelphia Museum of Art and showed me a book that contained *Nude Descending a Staircase*, but I could see no naked person. Nothing about this deal seemed right. Even the town's famous bell was broken.

When Mom and Dad left to go house hunting, Grams stayed with us. She bought me a book about Philadelphia, which had full-color photos and exuberant headings:

Cradle of liberty!

Freshwater port to the world!

Gateway to the enchanting Amish!

How could I not be enthused with all those exclamation points? I had been burned before ("Congratulations on selecting your new oboe!"), but this time there was an *army* of punctuation promises. I got jumping-jack crazy for Horn & Hardart Cafeterias! And Mummers! In Pennsylvania! Then the call came. Mom and Dad had bought a house. In New Jersey!

I was stunned. "I thought Dad's job was in Philadelphia."

"New Jersey is right across the river," Linda said.

Somehow, it didn't seem as glamorous. I'd be "adjacent" to the cradle of liberty, stuck in "the gateway to the gateway to the enchanting Amish."

Ginger reassured me. "New Jersey has the enchanting Mafia."

As moving day approached, I became even less enamored of the idea. I was about to be plucked from my universe that held our little colonial home, Good Shepherd Lutheran Church, Maury School, and my play area on the grand, sloping lawn of the towering George Washington Masonic Temple, which was built to resemble the lighthouse of Alexandria, Egypt. And what was to become of my betrothal to Pastor Beyer's 10-year-old daughter, Chris? We had planned our wedding and named our kids. I was a true sneak to walk out on her.

On a sad dawn just before Labor Day, we pulled away from the city, and I was determined to resist any positive coaxing.

"Wait till you see New Jersey!"

"It looks stupid on the map."

"We'll have to keep Taffy inside for a month. Otherwise he'll try to run back to Alexandria."

"Let him loose. I'll follow him."

During the brisk ride up Interstate 95, through the Baltimore Harbor Tunnel, across the Delaware Memorial Bridge and to the New Jersey Turnpike, I made sure Taffy scouted the terrain for our return trek.

"When do we see the Mafia?" I blurted.

Mom turned and looked at me. "The Mafia! Who told you about the Mafia?"

Ginger slunk down.

"They're cutthroats. And they can be anywhere." I informed my mother. "That's what we're getting into with this New Jersey thing."

Mom glared at Ginger.

"Well, *you're* always talking about the *Russians*," Ginger shot back.

"Don't get your mother started on the Russians," Dad said.

When we arrived I was blown away by our new house. It was a suburban split-level on a pie-shaped corner lot, just blocks from a lake. There were azaleas and a funny-looking mimosa tree out front. Mom panned the tan house color, which meant a bucket of turquoise paint was on the way. Inside, down to the left, was a spacious family room with sliding glass doors to a patio. Up to the right were the living room, dining room, and kitchen. On the next level were three bedrooms, including the master; a higher level had two more bedrooms, including Ginger's funky garret.

Dad traded in his Hillman Minx for a Chevy Biscayne, while Mom downsized from the Pontiac station wagon to a Corvair. When I ran into the garage to see it, Dad opened the hood and yelled, "Hey! Somebody stole the engine!" This bon mot, I'm sure, was whispered into the ear of every Corvair buyer as a sure-fire kid canard, but I, a graduate of the Glug Maker, did not bite.

Our neighborhood was filled with Olsons and Golds and Lazzerys and ethnic stores of all stripes. Soon I was sent to Longo's Market to buy cold cuts and sticky buns. I got my hair cut at Tony's Barber Shop. Tony spoke precious little English, and on our first visit, Dad tried to engage him with some friendly World War II stories. Dad learned posthaste not to mention "Mussolini" to an animated Italian who has clippers poised above his son's cowlick. I returned home shaken, with a lopsided "flat top" that sent my sisters into gales of laughter. I tried to press down the front of my hair with gobs of Brylcreem, but ended up looking like a cross between Lumpy Rutherford and Frankenstein's monster.

Near us, in Cherry Hill, was a place called a "mall" which had lots of stores under one roof. Its gurgling streams, exotic vegetation, and squawking macaws lulled you into such a stupor, you'd empty your wallet for high-end cheese, pink-haired troll dolls, or gag gift boxers with slits on both sides. To get to the mall you had to drive, literally, in circles. Six or more roads would feed into a "circle," where frightened drivers would zoom round and round till they could make it to their exit spoke, or, more likely, panic and dump off onto the wrong road. It was bumper cars for adults and great fun for nihilists and body shop owners.

This was a whole new world, and I had a thousand questions. One was, "Why does our address say *Oaklyn* when we live in *Haddon Township?*" The answer invited only more confusion.

If you live in Haddon Township, your postal address is *not* Haddon Township. Your address is another city, such as Oaklyn or Haddonfield or Collingswood. It could also be Westmont, which is a part of Haddon Township. The address for Haddon Township High School, for instance, is Westmont, NJ. We lived in the "Heather Glen" section of Haddon Township, and I went to sixth grade at Jennings School. But the stone monument out front said "Bettlewood School." In my class were "bus kids" from West Collingswood Heights, which is a noncontiguous section of Haddon Township with its own postal address.

None of this makes any sense. And even today, the people of Haddon Township, I am certain, stride blissfully to and fro, not knowing where they are or if a place called "Haddon Township" exists at all. In 1963, you certainly couldn't find it on a map. I just knew the Amish were two gateways away.

Not long after we arrived, a neighbor, Mr. Spang, told Mom and Dad he had three tickets to a twi-night doubleheader at Connie Mack Stadium. He was taking his son Jeffrey and wanted to know if I'd like to go. I was excited.

"Who's playing?" I asked Dad.

He checked the paper. "Let's see. On Friday, it's the Phillies and Dodgers."

"Cool."

"I used to go to the stadium as a kid," Dad said. "Back then it was called Shibe Park, and the Athletics were the big team. They even won the World Series."

"What about the Phillies?"

"Oh, nobody paid attention to them," Dad continued. "The A's were the ticket. The Phillies played in a ramshackle stadium called Baker Bowl before they moved to Shibe Park in the late '30s."

"Did you live near the stadium?"

"Nope. I'd jump on the trolley to North Philly and stand outside with a bunch of kids until the fifth inning, when they let us in for free. Connie Mack was the A's manager. He was a tall Irishman who knew how to build a team and win big."

"His real name was Cornelius McGillicuddy," Mom said.

"The A's moved to Kansas City in 1954," Dad said. "From then on, it was just the Phillies."

"Are they any good?"

"Your Aunt Nelle follows all the games," Mom said. "Let's give her a call."

"Wait till the rates go down!" Dad pounced.

Mom exhaled. "She'll be in bed."

"Well, we need younger relatives. When the rates go down, I want people who are up!"

After school on Friday, I was in Mr. Spang's car, speeding through Philadelphia. He wore sunglasses and had Lesley Gore's "It's My Party" cranked on the radio. I knew the song well, since Ginger had the 45. Her records had the initials "GW" painted on them in red nail polish—which meant hands off—but I sneaked them out of her room and danced to the hits.

Mr. Spang, the bespectacled Jeffrey, and I were tooling:

"It's my party, and I'll cry if I want to,
Cry if I want to, cry if I want to.

You would cry too—
MR SPANG: *Boo-hoo*
—if it happened to you."

We flew by row homes on Lehigh Avenue, where families sat on stoops craving the late-summer air. An African-American woman leaned out of her second-story window and hollered encouragement to three girls furiously working their hula hoops. I remember seeing black faces on billboards for the first time. The stadium, at 21st Avenue, was more majestic than I had imagined. Its ornamental French Renaissance façade was beautiful, even as it seemed to plead for a kindly buffing up that would restore its gracious, lady-like look of the early century.

Mr. Spang jumped out and made a brisk beeline for the building, as Jeffrey and I jogged to keep up. Inside, we fell into shady, concrete passages thick with people, and I was scooped up into the snaky flow, eye-level with carried cups of pungent brew and the occasional flicks of ash from dangling cigarettes. We walked through a short tunnel into a burst of light and color that stopped me cold; I plotted a course to my wooden seat as wide-eyed as if I were called to tea with the March Hare and Mad Hatter.

An expanse of very green grass, bright brown dirt, and important white lines were boxed in on three sides by canopied seats, flush with fans. On the fourth side, in right field, a tall, green-paneled wall completed the perimeter. Light standards rose high into the blue sky, their enormous bulbs pointing downward to the busy boys of summer who jawed and trotted and bent their knees for a go at pepper.

"They could have 30,000 here today," Mr. Spang said as we sat. "Sandy Koufax is pitching for the Dodgers."

I had heard of Sandy Koufax, so I knew he was important. I also liked how the name sounded and whispered it.

"Who's pitching for us?" Jeffrey asked.

"Chris Short in the first game," his dad answered. "I'm not sure about the nightcap."

"Dennis Bennett," a voice fell upon us.

We turned and saw a porky guy pinched into the row behind us. He was in his mid-20s, with a lazy right eye and questionable hygiene.

"He's 8 and 3, with a 2.60 ERA," he said quickly, as if delivering secret and vital information. "Better than last year's rookie stats of 9 and 9 and 3.81. Not a bad hitter either."

Lazy Eye grinned and continued his peanut shelling. We nodded thanks.

"The lineups are on the scoreboard," Mr. Spang pointed.

Lazy Eye leaned in. "That used to be the Yankees' scoreboard till they moved it here."

I turned around, interested, which was a mistake. I was not aware that tucked into the stands were blathering oddballs who might just as easily devote their Friday nights to stretching Swiss cheese or reading mattress tags.

"That's true about the scoreboard," Lazy Eye carried on. He picked a peanut skin from his teeth and sucked it back off his finger. "And see that wall in right field? Connie Mack put that up in the '30s to keep fans from watching the games from their roof! It's 40 or 50 feet high. The caroms off there go every which way, but Johnny Callison has it down to a science. And he's got the best outfield arm in baseball! He has more assists this year than Mickey Mantle, Willie Mays, and Roberto Clemente *combined*."

I then learned that the first All-Star Game under the lights was played here in 1943, during which his mother caught a ball which she later had autographed, but might now have to sell to help pay for her emphysema, which was her own damn fault for smoking too many Tareytons and was of less concern to him than his dog's butt-rubbing on the living room carpet. The guy was a flat-out filibuster.

Near us was a Connie Mack Stadium curiosity: one of dozens of seats throughout the park that had been placed *directly behind* a steel support girder, offering no view of the field. As Lazy Eye prattled, Mr. Spang nodded to the seat as a proper place for the gadfly, and Jeffrey and I laughed.

The Dodgers failed to score in the first, and Tony Taylor led off for the Phillies.

"He's from Cuba," Mr. Spang said.

I did a double take. "Doesn't he have to be from Philadelphia?"

Lazy Eye burst out laughing, hitting me in the head with potato-chip spittle. Mr. Spang tried to back him off with a stern look, but found it difficult to give the eye to someone with a lazy one. A comic bob and weave occurred, during which Mr. Spang became increasingly frustrated and my tormentor remained unchastened. By the third inning it became moot, as we heard a soda cup hit the deck and turned to find Lazy Eye snoring away, his belly bloated with treats. I felt a little sorry for him but was glad to be done with the stories of his dog's itchy ass.

I mulled the news that the Phillies were not born in Philadelphia. It was a startling revelation. GW football players, after all, were students at George Washington High School. But I was at an age of perpetual realization, so I went with it. Linda had just explained to me that the dollar bills Mom handed to the bank teller were not actually kept in a backroom box with Mom's name on it; in fact, none of the money deposited at a bank was kept in boxes with people's names on them. I looked at Tony Taylor and smiled: He and his mates had come from elsewhere, as I had.

Another thing clicked in me. I was always insistent on order; I liked knowing that everything in my room was in its proper place. Here, all the muscle and hustle of baseball—all of its force and motion—was played out on a neatly ordered landscape. As in the bottom of the seventh, when Bob Oldis engineered the perfect squeeze bunt that brought Don Hoak 90 feet from third to home for a 1-0

Phils lead. This was a game that made sense.

Sandy Koufax, as billed, was incredible. I could not believe how fast he pitched and how true he was to the tiny target of John Roseboro's mitt. Something about his cool confidence made me expect one good throw after another.

"He's pitching with only two days' rest," Mr. Spang said. "He can't pitch on the Jewish holidays next week, so he's going tonight to get the rotation back on schedule."

If Koufax was incredible, Chris Short was that and more. Koufax, lifted after seven innings for a pinch hitter, had eight strikeouts. But Short, his 6' 4" frame delivering fire, went the distance and had 14 Ks! In my first big league game, I saw not only a classic pitchers' duel, but also a rousing finish. Down 2-1 in the bottom of the ninth, the Phillies rallied to win 3-2, as Gene Mauch out-managed Dodgers skipper Walter Alston.

By the second game, Lazy Eye was up and bibbed for more chow.

"To the Phils!" he toasted loudly, raising a cup of Schlitz that he ceremoniously laced with two Alka-Seltzers.

A series of Vesuvian belches soon indicated that the plop-plop fizz-fizz had gone up against a mightier enemy, and I became increasingly concerned that I was stuck just south of imminent spew. When Mr. Spang called it a night after the third inning, I jumped up straightaway.

"Where ya going?" Lazy Eye demanded. "The '38 A's *played* seven doubleheaders in eight days and you can't finish one?"

I shrugged and waved goodbye.

"Hey!" he burped. "Come here."

I walked a few steps back. He pulled a stack of baseball cards from his pocket, sorted through them and handed me a Chris Short. I stared at it.

"You can have it—your first game and all. It's pretty rare to see somebody out-pitch Koufax."

"Thanks."

He held out his hand. As I went to shake it, he pulled away and chortled. I knew better. He was just a big softie.

That weekend, I was determined to be Chris Short. We went to Bristow's Sporting Goods, where Mom and Dad bought me a ball and glove and threw in a red Phillies cap. As I took up position at the end of our driveway, with one of the square garage-door panels as my target, it was evident there were flaws in my design. For one, Chris Short pitched *down* from a mound, and our driveway sloped *up* to the garage. Second, he was left-handed, and I was not. My career as a southpaw lasted less than two minutes while I hurled balls in all directions like a mad circus chimp. I switched hands and got pretty good at hitting the uphill strike zone with a fastball. Dad tried to teach me a curve, but I couldn't get any movement on the ball. So I went back to honing my basic throw, accepting that I'd be several pitches short of being Short.

I also bought a series of paperbacks about baseball stars and devoured the game's color. Minnie Minoso, I learned, got plunked more than any other batter and once played with a fractured skull. To this, he brought an all-part-of-the-game attitude: "You hit me and maybe I don't care so much. You hit my car, you got much trouble." Jimmy Piersall, a noted manic-depressive who had just run the bases *backwards* after his 100th career homer, was touted as a superb centerfielder, when he wasn't "browbeating umpires, kicking helmets, throwing baseballs at scoreboards and making stormy exits." Baseball's apocalypse would be upon us, I thought, if Piersall attacked Minoso's car. "Much trouble" would ensue.

More books arrived from Aunt Elsie and Aunt Nelle, and I was never so thrilled by history: The Babe's "called shot," Merkle's Boner, DiMaggio's 56-game hitting streak. There was no place crazier than Ebbets Field, no one braver than Jackie Robinson, no group loonier than The Gashouse Gang. As Dizzy Dean ran the bases in the '34 World Series, a ball plunked him in the noggin. The next day's headline read: "X-RAY OF DEAN'S HEAD SHOWS NOTHING." When

I discovered that Joe Nuxhall had broken in with the Reds at 15, I figured I had just five years to make the majors.

Stuffed with statistics, trivia and lore, I got ready for the 1963 World Series between the Dodgers and Yankees. Sandy Koufax was pitching in Game One, and I made every excuse to get out of school to watch it on TV. I began with a breathy, "I'm not feeling well," so lacking in thespian polish that Mom laughed for a good minute. She ignored, "Duchess ate my homework." She even rejected my most ingenious gambit: "I'm really not making any contribution to the class." Before leaving, I tried one last time, claiming I felt a little like Jimmy Piersall. She shoved me out the door.

When I got home, I heard that Koufax had struck out the first five batters—Tony Kubek, Bobby Richardson, Tom Tresh, Mickey Mantle, and Roger Maris—and, in a 5-2 win over Whitey Ford, set a Series record for single-game whiffs with 15. I got to watch Games Three and Four on NBC, and smiled broadly when I saw Koufax in the latter. "He looks just like he did at the stadium!" I proclaimed. He won Game Four with another sterling performance, and the Dodgers swept the defending champions.

Baseball had entered my life as surely as Italian-speaking barbers and Jersey accents, while much of the familiar remained, as I was reminded shortly after the Series. On the way upstairs, I heard Mom and Dad in a shouting match just inside their bedroom. Dad had invited someone from his office to dinner, and Mom was resisting. I couldn't get to my room without passing the set-to, so I detoured up another level to Ginger's. She pulled me inside.

"I couldn't get to my room," I explained.

"I know! Why do you think I took the room farthest from theirs?"

"That was smart."

I looked at her clothes and books strewn about, thinking she could be a tad more organized. She cleared a place for me to sit on the bed, taking special care with a photo of her boyfriend, Tom McClellan. He was the assistant pastor of our new church in Haddonfield, and the romance, according to Ginger, was "serious."

"I have news," she said. "I got Mom and Dad to pay for a dorm. I'm moving out in January!"

It was a jolt. Even though Susan and I were playmates and coupled as the youngest, Ginger was the sage, older sister I could trust, the achiever I could emulate. Her leaving was not good.

"What's college like?" I asked, sloughing over my disappointment.

"It's so amazing! I've decided to major in advertising art."

"You should fix the people in the Strawbridge & Clothier ads. They have no hands or feet."

"That's a style, silly," Ginger laughed. "How's *your* school going?"

"Fine. I like spelling and arithmetic."

"Have you made any friends?"

"I guess."

The truth was, I still felt like an outsider. My classmates were affable but showed little interest in my tales of Virginia. They also got tired of me asking about the Mafia. The lot of us, two dozen in all, would soon be linked, though, in a moment frozen by history. It was a perfectly ordinary fall afternoon when nothing but the next lesson was expected. It came, all right, but not from our books and with no kind regard for our innocence, which would soon be swept into waves of increasingly incomprehensible horror.

The classroom door opened and all heads turned. The principal, Mrs. Bennett, hurried in and whispered something to our teacher, Mrs. Holloway. Mrs. Holloway closed her eyes in distress. There was a pause, as if she didn't dare open them. When she did, she was direct.

"All of you go straight home," she said. "The president has been shot."

My first reaction, oddly, was that President Kennedy would be fine. I pictured the word "shot" as Ben Cartwright sitting in bed with a slinged arm, yucking it up with Hoss and Little Joe. I ran the long block home and found Mom in front of the television in the family room. Tears were streaming down her face. There were a hundred thoughts pounding in my head, but I flashed only on her fierce partisanship and uttered the most stupid words of my life: "Why are you crying over a Democrat?"

Mom did something she had never done. She reached back and slapped me, hard, right across the face.

"He was our president."

She took a long breath, exhaling sobs, and ordered me to my room. I stood there, smarting, and trying to process the word "was." I ran upstairs, turned on my Admiral radio and heard that President Kennedy had died. I felt horrible for what I had said. During the days that followed, our *family* room lived up to its name. The sad television pictures remain vivid today.

On Sunday, we watched a murder. Jack Ruby gunned down the suspected assassin, Lee Oswald. Dad leaped from his seat: "They shot him! Somebody shot him!" The chaos and shrill of the announcer's voice made my heart race. This was no episode of *Bonanza*.

We had little time to process the madness before the muffled drums of Washington touched us with grace. As six matching grays pulled the caisson carrying John Kennedy's coffin, as the darker, riderless horse bridled, as the cortege moved down Pennsylvania Avenue to the Capitol, Mom wept and Dad choked back tears. As people snaked to the rotunda to pay their respects, I thought of the line I had waited in with Ginger and Ruth in the same crisp air just 10 months before.

On Monday, there was no school. The reverent clop of horses to Arlington preceded a 21-gun salute, taps, and the lighting of the eternal flame. I kept a fix on Jacqueline Kennedy, whose eyes, though veiled, were far less mysterious than Mona Lisa's. They were filled with equal measure of grief and strength. When she was given the flag from her husband's coffin, I cried.

For weeks after, we lived in a somber fog. Chores were done, allowances were given, correct grammar was offered in class, but all with a robotic joylessness we had no power or desire to repel. Something more than a president had been taken from us, and sprightly steps or voices seemed subversive to the need for reflection. My funk went deeper: The images from Washington and Arlington made me homesick, I had made no fast friends in New Jersey, and Ginger would soon be leaving.

As I lay on my top bunk, with the gray of an afternoon pouring through the windows, I was grateful for Taffy's carefree purr. He was a handsome, mature tabby and wise, I thought, in his effortless ability to transcend all human concerns, despite our repeated insistence. I had held my View-Master to his eyes, but he was uninterested in the Colossus of Rhodes. Susan had crafted a house for him out of a cardboard box, complete with a "front door" for his convenience; he nonchalantly jumped out its "window." He had mastered the magic of being let in and out, served liver, and scratched under the chin, and unless he had been seen holstered on the Grassy Knoll, he had nothing to worry about.

I opened a book on the great lefty, Warren Spahn. Inside was a newspaper story Mom had clipped for me on the Phillies prospects for next year, and I re-read it. They had ended 1963 in fourth place, with a respectable 87-75 record, but were given little chance to compete with the National League's star-studded powers. The Dodgers had Koufax and Drysdale, the Giants trotted out Mays and McCovey, and the Cardinals featured the up-and-coming Bob Gibson, of whom Tim McCarver would say, "He's the luckiest pitcher I ever saw. He always pitched when the other team didn't score any runs." The Phils were a collection of journeymen and promising talent. And the weight of history was against them. Since their founding in 1883 (when they went 17 and 81), they had lost more games than any other major league team and had appeared in only two World Series, losing both. The 1961 squad set a record by dropping 23 games in a row.

However, I had seen Chris Short beat Sandy Koufax. And I knew something about underdogs. The doctor had been frank with Mom: *"We are going to try to pull you through this. Your baby will likely be lost."* But on the first day of spring, I was born alive and healthy. Mom told me this early on, she said, to make me a stronger boy.

When I read the article's conclusion, I smiled. Whatever the team's odds, it said, each spring is a blank slate when anything is possible.

After the most tumultuous year of my life, in the quiet aftermath of a national tragedy, "1964" suddenly seemed like a good thing to believe in. And so on a bleak, December day, with my wise cat as a witness, I made a pact that I have never broken.

The Phillies would be my team.

TAFFY'S HEAD

National League Standings Morning of September 24, 1964				
TEAM	WINS	LOSSES	PCT.	G.B.
Philadelphia	90	63	.588	--
Cincinnati	86	66	.566	3.5
San Francisco	85	68	.556	5
St. Louis	84	67	.556	5
Milwaukee	78	73	.517	11
Pittsburgh	77	73	.513	11.5
Los Angeles	75	77	.493	14.5
Chicago	69	82	.457	20
Houston	64	90	.416	26.5
New York	51	100	.338	38

The two windows facing my desk were open, and the smell of freshly cut grass filled the clear, autumn air. It was a pleasant place to do homework, which I undertook with earnestness in between long glances into our backyard of stubby trees and beyond to the neighbor's German Shepherd, Biff, who danced about at the end of his tether.

My room was efficiently laid out, with a piece of furniture on each wall: the bunk beds, where Taffy was balled up on high for his afternoon nap; a dresser; bookshelves; and the three-drawer, maple desk, which contained sharpened pencils, a protractor, and all other tools for serious study.

I had started seventh grade at Haddon Township Junior-Senior High School, which made me feel like an adult, especially since I got my own locker and walked the same halls as upperclassmen. I marched into math and Spanish and social studies with alacrity, hoping to continue the family tradition of high achievement.

One adventure I didn't bargain for was the list of items required for gym class, which included an "athletic supporter." Mom and Dad took me to Bristow's, and we picked out a red and white "Haddon Township" gym bag, plus shirts and shorts with the hawk logo. I wasn't sure what an athletic supporter was until the store attendant walked us over to them. When I saw the product illustration on the box, I froze. This was not a moment I wanted to share with my folks.

"They come in small, medium, and large," the attendant said brightly.

Mom looked away and Dad fidgeted. The male anatomy was not discussed at our house, and I was quite sure the mores of suburban Protestantism rarely allowed for the public cry, "Hey, my kid needs his first banana hammock!"

The clerk eyed me. "He looks like a medium."

"Are the small ones cheaper?" Dad asked.

"Same price."

"We'll take the medium," Dad said.

Then, I wished the store guy dead.

"On some of them, you can snap in a protective cup," he said. "The cup is extra."

The clerk pulled out a jock and demonstrated the cup insertion, as Mom turned redder than her hair.

"I'll wait in the car," she said, and vanished.

Dad quickly calculated the extra cost of the cup versus the odds of my nuts being crushed and declined the offer. With Mom gone, the whole thing put a little smile on his face, but I just wanted out of there.

In matters of anatomy, I had my own sources of information. One was the *Boy Scout Handbook*, with its cheery discussion of my sex organ. And I spent time in my room directly questioning my penis about its needs and motives. Not once did it demand to be shoved into a nylon pouch.

The first time I wore my new gear in gym class, however, Mr. Rosborough summed it up. "You boys need your jocks on," he barked. "When we do tumbling, I don't want anything tumbling out!"

Athletics were not yet up to speed at Haddon Township, which was a new school.

In football, we were consistently drubbed by our more established Colonial Conference rivals, especially Haddonfield and Collingswood. Our cheerleaders had three basic chants. The first would come a few minutes into the game, as our defense backpedaled:

"Hold that line! Hold that line!"

Invariably, one of our players would be plowed into the turf, and the second chorus would begin:

"Get up, Hawk, get up! Get up, Hawk, get up!"

As the opponent ran up the score, the final cheer would be offered:

"We've got spirit! We've got spirit!"

The most famous on-field exploit was engineered at halftime by a student bandleader who monkeyed with the sousaphone letters, H—T—H—S. He turned one "H" into an "I" and then rearranged his players. They marched down the field spelling, S—H—I—T.

Taffy got up, stretched, and deciding that was enough work for the moment, continued his slumber. Mom knocked on the open door and came in.

"How's it going?"

"Good."

She peeked at my book. "Looks like history."

"We're learning the Constitution."

"Pretty much the same one I learned," Mom said.

I nodded. "Mrs. Moldoff has a picture of Goldwater on one bulletin board and Johnson on the other. The loser gets taken down."

"Who are the kids for?" Mom asked quickly.

My classmates thought Barry Goldwater was kooky, but I shrugged, not wanting to upset her. Her door-to-door campaign was not going well, and it was pretty clear New Jersey would not be in the Republican column. Three years before, Goldwater had said, "Sometimes I think this country would be better off if we could just saw off the eastern seaboard and let it float out to sea."

So, what could Mom say when the neighbors opened up? "Hi! Vote for Goldwater, and we'll be on our way to Greenland!"

My shrug set her off.

"The Democrats have run things for 32 years!" she started in. "Except for the eight years Eisenhower was in office. And he wasn't really a Republican. He stole the nomination from Bob Taft."

I changed the subject. "Did you like my show last night?"

"It was good. I always thought you had a bit of the ham in you."

I smiled.

"And you'll have a bigger audience tonight," she said. "Nana's coming for dinner."

"Maybe she'll bring the Phillies luck."

Mom shuddered. "They need something." She eyed Taffy oddly and left.

Dad had to pick up Nana on the way home from work, and it

was 6:30 by the time he and his mother walked in. Tuna and noodle casserole, green beans, and warm, flaky rolls sat covered on the dining room table. In the living room, Linda and Susan played Fish, as Mom carefully placed the record player needle on "Moon River" for another sing-along with Andy Williams. Her voice was pitch-perfect; her eyes closed, lost in the melody.

I slumped in Dad's chair and glowered at the sports section. Under the banner, "RED-HOT REDS PUT HEAT ON HITLESS PHILS," there were two big pictures: Callison checking his swing on strike three and Taylor watching the ump call *him* out on strikes. There was a quote from Gene Mauch: "We had them—and let them get away."

I got up to greet Nana, who wore her usual big smile. She was short and plump and darkly tanned, and got about with a laborious waddle grounded in ugly black shoes. As Dad helped her up the steps to the living room, Duchess rushed to sniff her, and she whooped joyfully, "I love a dog! I love a dog!"

She clapped her hands, and Duchess wiggled excitedly.

"Yes, yes! Pretty doggie!"

"That's enough," Dad said to Duchess, gently shooing her with his foot.

"I should have brought doggie a gift!" Nana laughed, her childlike eyes darting about.

"Giving" was Nana's hobby. She needed no occasion to shower us with presents, usually the flashiest toy or whatnot in the store. She shipped us salt-water taffy from Atlantic City and once sent coconuts from Miami Beach that were nearly accompanied by a baby alligator before Mom and Dad got wind of it. Every Christmas, Mom pleaded with her to cut down on the gift-giving, but 12 months later, we'd see the largest haul ever. Whatever money she had, she spent gleefully.

Dad was her only child, and she raised him as a single mom. She owned a millinery store in downtown Philadelphia and made enough money selling hats to high-end customers to survive the

Depression. Mom claimed she coddled Dad, spoiled him rotten. All I knew was that she had one sweet heart. Her hands and arms followed that heart a little too severely: At any moment they could snatch you into a death hug.

Susan was already in her grip, pulled straight to the bosom, squeezed tight, and smothered so thoroughly that I could see only patches of orange hair and the silent scream of a bulging eye.

"Oh, my baby!" Nana cooed, rocking her quarry.

Susan choked on a dose of old lady talcum powder and struggled free, only to be yanked back into the vise.

The playful Ogden Nash once penned, "If called by a panther, don't anther." Had he grown up in our house, he might have opined, "It's frightening to ponda the dreaded Nanaconda."

Avoiding "Nanaconda" was an acquired skill; the trick was to anticipate when she might lunge and keep just beyond her tentacles. Lucky for me, she was probably the only person on the planet I could outrun.

After dinner, we settled into the living room for Thursday night's game. Mom adjusted the portable radio on the coffee table, while Nana plopped into the occasional chair next to the credenza. Duchess ran up to her and was instantly scooped into the big squeeze.

"I love you! Yes, I do!"

At the bay window, Taffy ceased his grooming and looked over in disgust. *Stupid, stupid dog.*

Duchess's capture may have been the biggest blow to canine pride since President Johnson showed off his beagles, Him and Her, and horrified the country by hoisting Him by the ears. Some columnist claimed Lady Bird was furious at LBJ. He said she told him that she, along with Him and Her, was upset by what her husband had done to Him. Lady Bird then said the reporter misquoted her and that he shouldn't speak for her or Him and Her. The whole thing degenerated into a he-said, she-said, Him-thought, Her-thought drama that entertained the public and, at least for a while, kept Dad's mind off the fact that the U.S. Postal Service was now charging *five cents to mail a damn letter!*

Nana was a casual baseball fan and seemed amused by our intense interest as the Phils opened a four-game set against the fifth-place Milwaukee Braves.

"Bunning is going tonight," Linda said. "So there are no excuses."

Nana applauded, letting go of Duchess, who fell in a heap and looked weakly at Taffy. *Smart, smart cat.*

Our veteran right-hander was gunning for his 19th win. He had won 10 out of his last 11, and 6 in a row at home. His mound opponent was 20-year-old Wade Blasingame, who had come up to the bigs just a year before. In the second inning, Bunning walked Eddie Mathews. The Braves catcher, Joe Torre, then lined the ball to center for a single, but it took a strange bounce over Adolfo Phillips and rolled for a triple, scoring Mathews.

"Can you believe it?" Dad raised his voice, slamming down the newspaper.

"This *is* ridiculous," Mom added.

"No breaks," Dad muttered.

In the Braves half of the fifth, Rico Carty singled. He was sacrificed to second, and the next batter fouled out.

"Their pitcher's up," I said happily. "Inning over!"

Blasingame stepped into the box. In another odd play, he broke his bat and blooped one into short right field, scoring Carty.

"Goddamn it!" Dad raged. He got up and walked into the kitchen.

We sat in a tense silence, until Nana leaned over to me.

"He never swore like that till the war," she said.

I nodded, and she nodded back, content to blame the whole episode on Hitler.

Dad returned with an ice cream sandwich and slumped into his chair. After another Braves single made it three-zip, he gritted his teeth. I had planned to entertain everyone with a new impression, but now was not the time. We were sullen as Blasingame took a one-hitter into the bottom of the seventh. When we finally got something going, Richie Allen had second base for sure, but over-slid and was tagged out. Moments later, Alex Johnson took second base safely, but made too wide a turn and was also thrown out. The Phillies had become the Keystone Kops.

"I'm telling you—this all started with Chico Ruiz," Dad sim-mered. "Right after that, the Reds pitcher balked and the umps didn't call it. That would have tied the game, 1-1. The next night, Short suddenly can't pitch. On Wednesday, Callison and Taylor are called out on strikes with the bases loaded. Taylor hardly *ever* strikes out. Tonight, it's bad hops and broken-bat RBIs. I could *tell* Ruiz was coming home. I could *just feel it*. That shook up every-thing, and now it's haunting the whole season."

There was an awkward pause before Mom spoke.

"Well, I'll tell you what it is."

She pointed to the bay window.

"It's Taffy."

All eyes shifted to Taffy, who was lounging on the sill.

"He's been sleeping on his head all week. That's bad luck."

"That means *rain*," Linda said.

"Rain. Bad luck. It's the same thing."

Nana jumped in. "Cats are sneaky. You never know what they're up to. That's why I like a dog."

"Oh, that's ridiculous," Dad scowled. "How can a cat control a baseball game?"

Taffy jumped down and walked out of the room, probably to get a lawyer.

"It may be an old wives' tale," Mom told Dad, "but it's just as pos-sible as your premonition. Some people live by the *Farmer's Almanac*."

"That almanac is a bunch of baloney," Dad insisted.

"A lot of players are superstitious," Linda said. "They wear lucky socks or whatever."

Dad was adamant. "I still say a cat can't control a game."

If life were fair, Taffy would have walked back into the room, pawed open the sports section and reminded us that the Detroit Tigers had won 80 games. Life being what it was, things got worse when the Braves scored twice in the eighth to make it 5-0. Nana wanted to go.

I helped Nana into the front of the Chevy Biscayne and hopped into the back. Dad, who was rarely a happy driver, was in a sour mood. As he tried to back out of the driveway onto Heather Road, a car passed by. Then another.

"It never fails," he shook his head. "There won't be a car all day, and the second I try to back out…"

On the White Horse Pike, he got stuck behind a slow driver.

"Look at this jerk!"

He passed the jerk and got trapped by another miscreant turning left.

"Left turns should be illegal!"

The road fed into a circle in Collingswood, and we barely escaped the horn-honking onslaught. Nana smiled nervously. I tried to focus Dad's attention on something else.

"Who are you voting for, Goldwater or Johnson?"

"Well, that's a good question," Dad said, racing to beat a red light. "For me, the issue is Viet Nam. I think Goldwater is reckless when he talks about using 'tactical' nuclear weapons."

He slowed the car to a respectable speed.

"I don't trust Johnson, either. He says he won't send our kids over there, but there's a build-up going on right now. We should stay out. We should learn from the French and just stay out."

Dad was ahead of the curve on Viet Nam, but he never did answer my question. I figured he'd vote for whoever promised to outlaw left turns. Sneakily, however, I had set the table for my newest imitation, a Texas-drawling LBJ. I leaned over the front seat and made a long face.

"Mah fella Ah-mericans. Ah'm announcin' tonight that if Mr. and Mrs. Wolfsohn ree-fuse ta vote fah me, ah will have ta pick each one up bah tha ears. First Her. Then Him."

Dad and Nana laughed.

"We've got a real comedian here," Dad said.

Nana pinched my cheek. "Just like Frank Gorshin. You could be another Gorshin!"

I did some more LBJ, and we were happier as we sailed into Camden. Nana and her sister, Nora, owned a small grocery store there, and they lived in the back, a dim space with linoleum floors and lumpy old chairs.

Dad scanned the run-down neighborhood as he pulled up to the store. When he got out, Nana turned to me.

"Your father's upset because he wants so badly to take you to a World Series."

She smiled and blew me a kiss.

Dad opened the door and helped her out. I sat there for a second and then did it without thinking. I jumped out of the car and walked straight to Nanaconda.

The hug was intense. But it never felt so good.

THE GREAT HAPPINESS

During the early months of 1964, our lives slowly returned to normal, though I thought often of President Kennedy's death and kept a closer eye on the news. But on a chilly winter day, I was just a boy with skates slung over my shoulders, rushing to the lake.

"It's frozen solid!" I shouted to a kid in mittens who stepped out of his house and looked skyward for the promised snow.

In moments, I was on the ice, jerky at first, hanging on to a cluster of laughing kids, falling with them in one hilarious pile. Then up, determined, righting my blades, sailing on adrenaline, fast and free. At the banks, a teenager ripped down the NO SKATING sign and hurried onto the ice for a victory lap. He weaved through the mob of us and hoisted the sign like Lord Stanley's Cup. We cheered. We made great ovals and figure eights and flew breathlessly through the flurries that filled the air, and I smiled at some feeling deep within. New Jersey had won me over.

To no surprise, I learned that the lake wasn't really a lake. It was Newton *Creek*, a wide runoff from Cooper River, which itself flowed into the Delaware.

When the weather warmed, we toured historic Philadelphia and learned that every important thing in the universe was discovered or invented by Ben Franklin, who was so wittily wise that he could make a leisurely meal out of hasty pudding. Soon after, we headed to Amish country. We got stuck behind an Amish couple going two miles an hour in their buggy; Dad broiled, but held his tongue and finally passed them without screaming, "Jerks are thee!" out the window. We stopped at a fair, and Mom bought a colorful hex sign.

"Will it put a curse on us?" Susan shrieked.

"No," Mom smiled. "The hex sign brings *good* luck."

Perfect. Next winter I would rub the hex sign for luck before skating on the lake that was a creek in my hometown of Haddon Township that the post office called Oaklyn. Maybe Mom would keep the hex sign in her car, which had its engine in the trunk.

My birthday came and went and brought with it the change of seasons. Spring training was under way in Florida, and nothing seemed so welcome as the crack of a bat, the hubbub of a casual crowd or the hopeful mumbles of rookies in camp. Finding WFIL on my transistor radio, however, required the steady hand of a Swiss watchmaker. One slight movement of the tiny dial and I'd hear Jimmy Gilmer and The Fireballs; a jerk in the other direction and I'd catch the latest diatribe by Cambodian Prince Norodom Sihanouk:

The Phils getting a good look at young Danny Cater, who … got to get back to that sugar shack … has demanded reparations from the United States for the attack … to that sugar shack … on Cambodian soil by what he called imperialist powers and their South Vietnamese puppets … now that sugar shack queen … will call for an investigation by the U.N. Secretary General … who was signed as a shortstop but may get a start or two in the outfield.

By the time I got tuned into the game, I was only slightly confused.

"Who's the new kid in left field?" Dad asked.

"U Thant!" I replied.

The Phillies (with or without the Burmese Secretary General—I still am not sure) plodded through Grapefruit League play with a so-so record, but remained dutifully optimistic. In the off-season, they had traded with Detroit for two veterans, pitcher Jim Bunning and catcher Gus Triandos. Bunning was the marquee catch, an All-Star who had already won 118 games in the Junior Circuit. There were plenty of promising rookies, too, chief among them Richie Allen, a muscular and strong-willed Pennsylvania kid who had torn up the minors and quickly beat out Don Hoak for the third base job.

On Opening Day, the Phillies played at night, and I accepted the contradiction without comment. As 21,000 filed into Connie Mack Stadium for the contest against Casey Stengel's Mets, Dad puttered in the garage, half-interested: "The Phillies are usually so bad, people show up on Opening Day with signs that say, WAIT TILL NEXT YEAR!"

In my room, I paced through the pre-game show and hoped for the best. The best came quickly as Roy Sievers got the Phils going with a three-run homer in the first.

"All right!" I shouted, jumping up and down on the hardwoods.

Mom passed by with a basket of laundry.

"What's the ruckus?"

"Three nothing Phils already!"

"Good for them. But it's a long season, so don't wear out your Keds tonight."

The story of the evening was brilliant defense. Tony Taylor stretched out, snared a hard grounder and turned it into a double play to break up a Mets threat in the third. Richie Allen speared a ball in the fourth to kill another Mets rally and began a sparkling double play in the fifth. In the seventh, Danny Cater made an incredible one-handed catch against the left field wall. The Phillies won, 5-3.

In the next game, Jim Bunning struck out 11 Mets in his National League debut. Our centerfielder, Tony Gonzalez, blasted a three-run homer in the eighth to break a 1-1 tie and propel the Phils to a 4-1 victory.

In Game Three at Wrigley Field, pitcher Art Mahaffey was the hero. At bat with two on, he caught a 25-mph jet stream and sent one over the ivy, as we out-slugged the Cubs, 10-8.

I always liked numbers, and three three-run homers in the first three games seemed like an omen. Sure enough, an undeniable spirit took hold, with Mauch prowling the dugout and everyone contributing. Allen had two round-trippers to help beat the Cubs, 8-1. John Herrnstein's two-run double capped a four-run ninth as the Phils rallied to stun the Pirates, 6-5. Gonzalez drove in four runs to pace a 16-hit attack as we routed the Cubs, 10-0. Shortstop Bobby Wine launched a three-run shot to down the Cubs again, 5-1. In a 4-2 triumph over the Reds, Allen raised his batting average to a sizzling .442, with a homer, triple, and two singles. Dennis Bennett tamed the Reds with a complete game, 3-1. Bunning stayed unbeaten with a 5-3 win over Warren Spahn and the Braves.

Suddenly, the Phils were 10 and 2 and sitting atop the National League.

As I trotted outdoors and smacked a Wiffle ball high into the sky of racing clouds, there was no suppressing my joy. Come game time, radios clicked on everywhere in our house and, it seemed, everywhere in the neighborhood. The *Phillies* were the ticket ... or as Tony the Barber told me, "They is real fantastic good." We drove to a Saturday game, and I skipped to my seat as if I owned the place.

"They put up that wall so people couldn't see for free," I told Mom and Dad. I looked around for Lazy Eye. "They played an All-Star Game, and this guy's mother was here, but now she has some disease that makes her rub her butt on the carpet."

I had only recently slipped the word "butt" into conversation without some reprimand. "Ass" would surely get me grounded.

"I saw a lot of great games here," Dad carried on. " The A's could out-pitch and out-hit anyone. There was one month when Jimmie Foxx, Mickey Cochrane, and some other guy all hit for the cycle."

"Paul and Lloyd Waner ruled the outfield in Pittsburgh," Mom jumped in. Paul could hit doubles like nobody's business."

Man, they seemed happy. I decided to test it.

"I think I got it wrong. It wasn't this guy's mother. It was his *dog* who rubbed his ass on the carpet."

"Dogs'll do that," Dad said.

He hollered as the Phils took the field. This was unbelievable. I could get away with *anything*. By the fourth inning, I was more intrigued by my folks than the game. Something in those wooden seats or the flight of a baseball had lifted them into a great happiness.

I poked Dad. "When you met Mom, did you know she was a Pirates fan?"

"All I thought was, *'Who is that beautiful redhead from Pittsburgh?'*"

Mom smiled. "He came over to help make some posters. But I could tell he had other things on his mind."

"I wasn't going to let the prettiest girl in Washington get away." She glowed.

This was too rich. *Butt. Ass.* I was sitting on a gold mine.

"Could I have some cotton candy?"

Dad shook his head. "Remember, we still have a bridge toll to pay."

Heaven on earth had its limits.

By mid-May, the Phillies were locked in a seesaw battle for first with the San Francisco Giants. It was then that The Great Happiness would be tested when Grams arrived for a week's visit. Her lordliness always brought out the insecurity in Dad, with Mom caught in the middle. In the old days, I could've made a few nickels off it.

Whenever Grams walked in, she turned her cheek and Dad planted a fake kiss on it; they generally ignored each other until dinner, when the catty volleys would begin.

DAD (to the table): "Took forever to get to work on the Schuylkill Expressway. The old 'Sure Kill.'"

GRAMS (chuckles): "Well, too bad you couldn't hold onto your job in Washington, Hal."

DAD (chokes on asparagus): "That's okay. Traffic picked up once I got on *Roosevelt* Boulevard."

GRAMS (sucks air): "Well, if it's a good road, I'm sure they named it for Teddy. (to Linda) Teddy was the finest president since Lincoln."

DAD (to Grams): "Didn't you know Lincoln personally?"

GRAMS: "I might have. But he was shot by John Wilkes Booth, (to Linda) *a man who couldn't hold onto a job in Washington.*"

MOM (to me): "Stop feeding Duchess!"

On *this* visit, Dad was wrapped up in the pennant race. Moreover, he seemed downright chatty with Grams, which kept her so off balance she found herself sitting among us following baseball and a little moment for the record books.

In Houston, Chris Short was pitching a 1-0 shutout in the fifth. The Colts' Rusty Staub was on second and Walt Williams was on first. Jerry Grote hit one to first baseman John Herrnstein. Herrnstein flipped it to second to force Williams, and the return throw got Grote at first. Staub rounded third and headed home, but Herrnstein nailed him with a perfect throw to Gus Triandos.

"Triple play!" Dad screamed, scaring the bejesus out of Grams. We whooped it up.

"Such clamor," Grams said.

"Why don't you show Grams your room?" Mom suggested.

I took her up.

"Triple plays are really rare," I bubbled. "Everything in baseball comes down to a number, like batting averages."

"Well, perhaps that will help with your mathematics."

I knew what Grams and I had in common, and I made a shameful play for approval.

"Do you like my room?"

"Yes!" She clapped her hands. "Everything is so nicely arranged.

Your bed is made and your books are all put away."

I walked over to the shelves. "I got the *Book of Knowledge* from Ginger. I put the large books over here, and the rest are stacked according to height."

"Very nice," she said. "You could also arrange them alphabetically by the author."

"Maybe I will."

Grams smiled. "Your grandfather would have been very proud of you."

"I never had a grandfather. Dad's father died when he was a baby."

"Well, you have two grandmothers who love you."

She had said the perfect thing.

When I got home from school the next day, Mom and Grams were out back on our aluminum lawn chairs. Mom nestled in and cradled a glass of iced tea. Grams, who stared at the chair's green and white nylon webbing as if it were some cheap, proletarian horror, smoothed her floral dress and made the best of it. I picked up the paper and scanned the box score.

"A 2-0 shutout! RBIs by Covington and The Pope."

Instantly, I knew I'd stepped in it.

Grams frowned. "The Pope?"

"It's a nickname for Tony Taylor," I said, fidgeting. "Aunt Nelle calls him The Pope."

"Why does she call him that?"

I hesitated.

"Why does she call him The Pope?"

"When he comes to bat," I confessed, "he crosses himself."

Grams exhaled.

"You see," she fussed at Mom. "The Catholics are everywhere. Now you can't even walk into one of these baseball parks without them making a public display of their doctrine. First, the government puts fluoride in the water, now this!"

The neighbor behind us, stocky Mrs. Manuel, waved as she hung out laundry, and Mom motioned her over to meet Grams. The Manuels owned the Oaklyn Bakery, so I made a point of staying on their good side since I was always a few cents short when ordering their cream-filled doughnuts—my favorite.

Grams stood to shake hands, which put her about eye level with the crucifix hanging from Mrs. Manuel's neck. Mom and Mrs. Manuel chitchatted, as beads of sweat popped up on Grams's brow. She reached into her bosom, site of the world's largest tissue factory, and pulled out a wad. She dabbed her forehead with it, then reached in for another, then another. Had she been a magic act with rabbits in there she could have owned the Poconos. As I looked back and forth between her face and the rood, it was hard to tell who was more tortured, grimacing Grams or jewelry Jesus. A yelp away from yanking out her entire brassiere, she excused herself and hustled inside.

By dinnertime, when Ginger arrived with her boyfriend, Grams looked like a dazed featherweight. Mom told Dad what happened, and a mischievous grin lit his face. He had home field advantage.

Grams rose and Ginger kissed her before announcing, "This is Tom."

Grams regained her smile. "The assistant pastor!"

"No. Tom is a Marine."

Mom explained. "She was getting too serious with Tom *Mc-Clellan* —"

Grams was confused.

"— so she's dating other boys."

Ginger braced. "This is Tom Donohue."

"*Donohue?*" Grams blinked and gave him the once-over. "That's Irish, isn't it?"

"Irish *Catholic*," Dad smiled.

Grams went numb and gave out a horrible whimper. She listed momentarily and then wobbled like a grazed bowling pin. Mom tried to grab her.

"Mother!"

Grams collapsed.

"Help me! Get her to the couch!"

Ginger laid her down.

"Put a pillow behind her head," Mom said.

"If that doesn't work," Dad helped, "there's a sack of Pillsbury flour in the cupboard."

Grams moaned.

Dad loved it. "Does she need last rites? Somebody get a priest!"

Mom shooed him away.

"Mother," she said, patting Grams's cheeks, "Tom is a Republican!"

Ginger waved over Tom. "Tell her you're for Goldwater!"

Tom froze, as if he'd been dropped into a pit of crazies. Ginger hauled him over.

"Yes," he assured her. "I'm backing Barry."

Her eyes rolled to the back of her head.

"Everyone clear the room," Mom said. "She needs to rest."

"Poor Grams," poor Linda said.

She'd been knocked to the mat by The Pope, a crucifix, and her granddaughter's Irish boyfriend. The old Vatican triple play.

Grams recovered, of course, and gave Mom hell for letting Ginger date a non-Lutheran. Mom wasn't keen about it either, but let Grams's Protestant protest roll off her back. And The Great Happiness held. As the Phils took the first two games of a three-game set at Dodger Stadium and led the league with a 21-12 record, Mom and Dad seemed jubilant. They were even going on a *date*.

As they got ready, I sat downstairs with Grams and got brave.

"Why don't you like Catholics?" I asked.

She arched her back. "Don't you know your history? What have they taught you in Sunday School?"

I shrugged.

"Martin Luther started the Reformation because the Catholics were corrupt. They let people buy their way into heaven by selling indulgences. They stifled science, tortured dissenters, and even killed thousands of cats! Martin Luther stopped this nonsense of going through a *priest* to get to God. You don't need a priest to speak to God, do you? You just put your hands together and pray. You should stay away from Catholics and anything that smacks of Rome!"

Mom and Dad bounded to the door, dressed up.

"Where are you going?" I asked.

"To a swanky nightclub," Mom said.

Grams recoiled. Her daughter had referred to a "nightclub" and modified it with the word "swanky."

"What's it called?" I asked.

Dad winked. "The Latin Casino!"

Grams threw up her hands, as if it were another thing she just couldn't control. I took her to my room, and we had a swell time alphabetizing my books by the author.

A PURSE FULL OF FISH

National League Standings Morning of September 25, 1964				
TEAM	WINS	LOSSES	PCT.	G.B.
Philadelphia	90	64	.584	--
Cincinnati	86	66	.566	3
St. Louis	86	67	.562	3.5
San Francisco	85	68	.556	4.5
Milwaukee	79	73	.520	10
Pittsburgh	77	75	.507	12
Los Angeles	75	78	.490	14.5
Chicago	70	82	.461	19
Houston	64	90	.416	26
New York	51	100	.338	37.5

"We've got a real comedian here."

Dad's words echoed in my head as I walked to school along Cuthbert Boulevard, a busy, hilly thoroughfare. Was it true? Was I a comedian?

On Wednesday, my coffee table shenanigans were spontaneous. But for Thursday, I planned an LBJ bit and chose the perfect time to deliver it. The thought of President Johnson picking up Mom and

Dad by the ears was funny. I could see it in my head. Dad and Nana laughed, so they got the idea, too. Of course, it crossed my mind that the Secret Service could appear out of nowhere and hustle me into a limo, where I'd face a furious LBJ: "Some of mah fella Ah-mericans have takin' ta jokin' 'bout me. And here's what happens ta them!"

A panel would open to reveal a sniveling seventh grader whose ears had been stretched to the size of Dumbo's.

But no matter. I was getting attention and I liked it. Maybe I'd even get a double allowance. And what was wrong with laughing anyway? Our team needed a win, and we were all on edge.

The least happy member of the household was Taffy. When I got home from school, he was outside, uncommonly annoyed.

"What's wrong?"

I can't get any sleep, that's what's wrong. Every time I curl up on my head, the big lady nudges me awake. I was having a sweet dream that I was running high-grade catnip for the Cosa Nostra, pushing 50 kilos a day. Then I was rudely aroused.

"Mom's trying to figure out what's wrong with the Phillies."

They're tired! Take a look at the sports section. Chris Short is pitching tonight on two days' rest.

"You read the sports section?"

What else do I have to do? I can't SLEEP! By the way, there's an ad for a bathrobe on page 30. I want it.

"You don't wear a bathrobe."

I want the box. To SLEEP IN!

"All right. I get your point."

Hey, I hear you're a comedian now. So tell me a joke.

"Okay. What do you and the 1919 World Series have in common?"

What?

"You were both fixed."

Oh, please. Every tom in the neighborhood has heard that one. Classy comedy is when the punch line hits when you least expect it.

"What do *you* know about comedy?"

I almost went onstage. But I didn't have the balls.

I laughed.

See. Now THAT'S funny!

"Maybe we should team up."

I'll sleep on it. Got any suggestions WHERE?

Inside the house, I read the paper. The Phillies had battled back Thursday night. With the Braves ahead 5-0, they scored three runs in the eighth on a two-run single by Callison and another RBI single by Allen. Still, it was a 5-3 loss, and with the Reds idle, our lead was trimmed to three games. Meanwhile, St. Louis swept a doubleheader from Pittsburgh to move into third place.

It seemed like everyone had a remedy for the faltering Phils. My favorite was Aunt Nelle's.

"Mauch should take the boys out," she told me on the phone, "and get 'em soused. They're too tight. If they play with a hangover, they won't even know it's September. The Babe was liquored up half the time and it didn't cripple him. Why don't those knuckleheads in the front office answer my letters? They should send the boys out on a bender, I tell you. Ask your mother to bring me some Chiclets on Sunday, for I've chewed up a couple of boxes listening to the nightly farce at Shibe Park."

It was Friday, which meant dinner at Howard Johnson's. They had an all-you-can-eat fish buffet, and Dad had us lined up for a table before most Catholics were even in the parking lot. I had to admire the planning and industry that went into Dad's effort to stretch a buck. We were encouraged to make multiple trips through the line and pile our plates high with haddock, all the while lectured about the poor kids in China who barely had the strength to drag a pail of turnips through the muddy streets.

As I stuffed my mouth with breaded fillets, talk turned to the Phils.

"Why are they pitching Short on two days' rest?" Dad complained, as he flagged the waitress with an empty ketchup bottle. "Why not go with Culp?"

"Down the stretch, you go with your best," Mom replied.

"Your best with *rest*," Dad insisted.

"Mauch knows what he's doing," she countered.

I looked at Dad. "Have you seen the mayor about tickets?"

"Let's hit the line again," he said.

"I'm full."

"Come on," he insisted.

This was the part I hated. Bloated, we had to trudge through the line for our "to go" fish.

"Could I get more napkins?" Dad asked the waitress when we returned.

He quickly became Steve McQueen in *The Great Escape*. Mom had to wrap each fillet in a napkin and stuff them into her purse without attracting the attention of other eaters or the manager, an earnest goof who wore a white shirt and thin, black tie.

"I can't fit it all," Mom grumbled.

"Sssshhhhh!" Dad said. "Keep packing."

"We're out of napkins," Mom said.

"Damn!" Dad whispered.

Had he and Grams not been mortal enemies, they'd have made a great team. He could scan for the HoJo Police as she wrapped his stolen fish in an endless supply of bosom tissue.

On the way home, Dad whistled happily. Mom looked at him and shook her head.

"Johnson should send you to deal with the Russians. They'd find their vodka gone in five minutes and surrender."

Dad lifted his hand in a toast. "Here's to peace!"

In the back seat, Linda leafed through my scrapbook of box scores.

"We haven't dropped more than four straight all year," she said. "Losing tonight would be a catastrophe."

Mom in 1942 when she worked at the War Department. She claims to have spurned the advances of many officers, including a general.

Me in 1958 with the "giant stuffed giant panda."

Dad in England before D-Day. Considering how many times we were lost driving, I am amazed he crossed the English Channel in the right direction.

With Nana in Alexandria after the Cuban Missile Crisis in 1962. It felt great not to have been evaporated!

Our house in Haddon Township, NJ. To understand why our postal address was Oaklyn, you'd have to read the Borough Act of 1878.

My sixth grade class at Jennings School. I helped draw the flames on the doomed Spanish Armada. On November 22, 1963, Mrs. Holloway told us that the president had been shot.

Dad, Linda, Susan, me, and Mom in 1964. I love Linda's hair. She didn't even need to buy a Beatles wig!

Ginger and Tom and The Great Catholic Scandal of 1964!

My seventh grade photo (1964-1965) at Haddon Township Junior-Senior High School. Don't even ask why its postal address is Westmont.

Taffy and Duchess on
Dad's olive leather recliner,
waiting for the Phillies
broadcast to begin.

Grams, ever the detective,
could sniff out a Roosevelt
dime at thirty feet.

Aunt Elsie with Mutt.
"Snap...crackle...pop!"

Aunt Nelle and
Aunt Vicki outside
their apartment in
Harrisburg. It was
always dangerous to
keep Aunt Nelle on
a public sidewalk for
very long.

COURIER-POST

SPORTS

CAMDEN, N. J., FRIDAY, AUG. 23, 1963   25

BILL DUNCAN

Ashburn Has No Regrets
Over Decision to Retire

Richie Ashburn has no regrets over leaving the ranks of active players to become a baseball broadcaster.

The 36-year-old blonde, popular former outfielder has been a play-by-play announcer and color man this season for the Phillies games with Byrum Saam and Bill Campbell, veteran pros, as his companions.

Last season Ashburn hit over .300 for the lowly Mets and many fans felt he was foolish not to continue his active career until he fell considerably below .300. Ashburn doesn't agree.

"Up in the broadcaster's booth I get the feeling once in awhile I still should be playing," said Richie. "But not as often as I thought I would. Frankly, I'm surprised I don't miss it more.

"I like broadcasting as much as I did playing. First of all it's a baseball job, not a playing job, but I'm seeing all the games and voicing opinions. It's a challenge."

Hitting the ball is what Ashburn misses most of all. Never a power hitter, he was a good singles and doubles man and twice led the National League in percentage, in 1955 with a .338 and in 1958 with .350.

"When I study some of these pitchers from the booth I'd like to go down there and take a whack at the ball," he said.

Ashburn feels he could have played several more years and "have been some kind of an asset to a ball club" but he thought there was a youth movement in New York and he would have been benched.

RICH ASHBURN

At it turned out, the acquisition of Duke Snider and the regular play of Frank Thomas proved the Mets were not concentrating on youth in their outfield.

* * *

Richie works out on the field every day before a game, mostly pitching to the batters. Also catching. Many fans didn't know it but Ashburn was a catcher-outfielder for Utica in the Eastern League in 1945. He says most players are suspicious of sportswriters and casters, but he doesn't consider himself under suspicion as yet. Asked to explain, he said he meant players fear finding what they say will be in print or broadcast over the air the next day.

Ashburn said he finds himself defending blunders by players over the air, especially mental blunders. He cited the instance of Clay Dalrymple forgetting there were two outs.

"I've done that myself," he said. "So I could feel for Clay."

We discussed his many great days with the Phillies, his throw which saved the pennant in 1950 and other dramatic moments. We agreed one of the high points was the final day of the 1958 season. Richie was in a hot duel with Willie Mays for the batting championship.

* * *

Bob Skinner of the Pirates made a shoe string catch and deprived Richie of a hit his first time up. He hit safely his second and third times at bat. In the press box we wondered why he didn't play it safe and quit with two out of three. But he came to bat two additional times, drawing a pass and hitting safely again for three hits in four official times at bat. Mays was three for five, we later learned over the ticker and Richie was the batting champion. He had refused to play it safe and had won. Every hit was clean. There was no tough decision for the official scorer.

* * *

Despite his two batting championships and his lifetime average of .308, Ashburn will best be remembered for his defensive work. Thousands of fans from New Jersey and Philadelphia will never forget him racing to the far recesses of Connie Mack Stadium and pulling down a hard hit ball that, when it left the bat, seemed destined for extra bases.

Richie Ashburn, now in the Hall of Fame, was the speaker at our church's father-son dinner in 1963, and I got his autograph.

Monday Morning
10 August 1964

Dear Carl.....

Hi honey. How're you doing?
Bet you are having a good time. Is
it cold there at night ....and how's
the sleeping bag?

We are freezing '..... fire in
the fireplace day & night. The
temperature here at 9:00 this
morning is 49°! Our cabin is
nice, & the lake is beautiful,
but so far it has been too cold
to go in the water.

I heard the Phillies won
Sat. & Sun ..... did you hear the
games? Hope they keep winning.
We're sort of isolated here......your
radio comes in handy. We get a
Canadian station, & they rotate
programs in English, french, Spanish

& Italian. We hear the ball
scores at the end of the day & coming
up we heard the Red Sox - Chicago
game on radio.

Your sisters are having a
good time ..... Susan did write
to you & Ginger & Linda will
be writing also. Be a good boy.....
be careful in the water & take
it easy! We miss you lots.
Say hello to Rusty for us, & to his
parents when you see them. Did
you run out of money yet? Here's
an extra dollar, but don't spend
it all on candy. Are you eating
the camp food? We'll be
anxious to hear from you. Bye for
now.

Love & Kisses...

Mom's letter to me
during Boy Scout
summer camp.

My *1964 Phillies Yearbook.* The third edition featured Jim Bunning's perfect game on Father's Day.

The Phillies pennant Dad bought for me at the "Chico Ruiz"
game on September 21, 1964.

Mom with Pete Rose at spring training in Clearwater, FL in 1983.
She had done a story on him for *American Astrology* magazine.

"Well, good news," Mom chirped. "Taffy hasn't slept on his head all day."

"He could be on it now," Linda warned.

Mom turned around. "Mrs. Manuel is keeping an eye on him." Taffy was up against informants.

"It might be *me* bringing them bad luck," I announced. "So I'm not going to listen to the game tonight."

Linda rolled her eyes. "Why don't we go live in a bomb shelter?"

I spent the night tucked away, practicing impressions. One of my favorites was Mrs. Drysdale, whose obsession with the Clampetts kept her on the verge of a nervous breakdown. I had her down, too. "Those dreadful hillbillies!" I'd shiver, before collapsing onto the floor in a dead faint. "Those dreadful hillbillies!" I'd holler and land on the throw rug. It was the fainting part I liked.

On occasion, I would spruce up the tantrum with wardrobe, which consisted of my Beatles wig, from which I hung two Erector Set pulleys as earrings. Soon, Duchess was drafted into the act to play Mrs. Drysdale's poodle, Claude. I would lead her around my room on a leash and then halt dramatically. "What is it, Claude? Oh, no! It's those dreadful hillbillies!" And down I'd go. Duchess quickly tired of the affair, choosing her chew bone over a pitch for Hollywood fame. I immediately replaced her in the act with an uncooked hot dog. Any in-depth assessment of this snapshot from my youth—an 11-year-old boy wearing a bejeweled wig and dragging a leashed sausage—would surely cost me $100 an hour, but I am quite content to remember it as budding theater.

If I *were* a comedian, as Dad said, I'd have to work harder. I'd have to write some bits. While I liked order, I realized that comedy often came from disorder: "Those dreadful hillbillies" moving to L.A. or Lucy sneaking into Ricky's act or a sergeant, like Bilko, outsmarting a colonel.

Tonight, I got the idea that Granny Clampett would try to cure the Phillies with her moonshine. It went something like this: Granny scampers toward Gene Mauch as Jed tries to stop her. In the crowd, Mrs. Drysdale freaks out. *"Milburn! It's those dreadful hillbillies!"* Granny corners Mauch. *"I come to doctor yer boys with my baseball medy-cine."* Jed intervenes. *"Don't take it, mister. She gave a sip to Jimmy Piersall, and he ain't been right ever since."* The Phils down her jug and go berserk, climbing the backstop. Granny hightails it. *"Jeeeeeeeeed! Jeeeeeeeeeeeeeeeeed!"* The Connie Mack crowd boos yet another grandmother. The lit players moon the crowd. Mrs. Drysdale screams and faints. *"Those dreadful Phillies!"*

I practiced the skit in the mirror, with saucy regard for the curtain dropper:

"Those dreadful Phillies!"

On my fourth faint, I looked up and saw Susan.

"You are so weird."

"I am not!" I burped. "I'm trying to do Mrs. Drysdale without barfing up my HoJo's."

I got to my feet.

"Good news," Susan said. "The Phillies are ahead, 1-0."

"Yes!"

"Why is there a hot dog on your desk?"

"It's part of the act."

"If Dad finds a hot dog missing, you'll be in trouble."

"Go away!"

After she left, I hid the hot dog. Time passed tortuously. I looked up a few dirty words in the dictionary. I heard cheers in the living room, and several moments later, Mom popped in. I slammed the dictionary shut on "glans."

"It was 3-1 Braves in the bottom of the eighth, but Callison hit a two-run homer to tie it!" she gushed.

"Yay!"

Not long after, she was back.

"Still 3-3. They're going to extra innings."

This was excruciating. And I started to over-think. What if the

Phils won? Would it prove I was bad luck? Or was it Taffy? Would I have to avoid the rest of the games? If I showed up at the World Series, would they lose? Would the crowd boo me like a grandmother? Why was the head of my penis called a glans?

It was late, and all I wanted was the Phillies to win. I sat by the door and listened breathlessly for hoopla or heartache. I dozed off.

There is nothing so wondrous as the moment you awake and find yourself in your dreams. There was jubilation downstairs. Unbridled joy. In extra innings, it could mean only one thing: The Phils had done it! I was hardly standing when Dad pushed open the door.

"Richie hit an inside-the-park home run! Cookie singled and Richie hit one off the scoreboard! It rolled past the centerfielder and he made it all the way!"

I leaped halfway to the moon. "We won!"

"No, no, no," Dad said. "The Braves already scored two in the tenth, but this ties it. 5-5!"

I nearly crapped my Howard Johnson's. What word could I pluck from Webster's to describe this agony?

Later, as our cuckoo clock showed just before midnight, I stood at the top of the stairs and gleaned the horror. The Braves had scored two in the twelfth to win, 7-5. The Reds were sweeping a doubleheader from the Mets, melting our lead to a mere one and a half games. Linda passed me on the way to her room and managed a weak whisper.

"Well, it wasn't you, and it wasn't Taffy."

Downstairs, Mom and Dad struggled with the postmortem.

"I told you Short would be no good on two days' rest!"

"That's nonsense," Mom argued. "He pitched into the eighth and gave up only one earned run. Mauch was right to pitch him."

Dad paced.

"They're fighting hard," Mom kept on. "Allen had three hits yesterday and four tonight. We're just not getting any breaks."

"It was that damn interference call against Dalrymple," Dad

fumed. "Without that, we'd have won 2-1. How many times does an *interference call* decide a game? I'm telling you—we've been cursed *ever since Monday!*"

"They'll figure it out. Mauch will figure it out."

"You and Mauch. You should marry the guy."

If Mom married Mauch, I thought, I'd get to see a lot more games.

"All right," Mom said. "I admit we're jinxed. But getting upset isn't going to help. Just calm down."

"Don't tell me to calm down!"

"Fine. Then don't calm down."

Dad grabbed his keys and stomped towards the door.

"Where are you going?" Mom shouted.

He left. I heard the door slam and a car tear out of the garage. The Great Happiness had taken one in the gut.

I tiptoed downstairs. Mom was on the sofa, head back, eyes closed. I glanced at a stack of newspapers on the coffee table and saw an ad from earlier in the week. Some guys were clutching their drinks, and the copy read, "Make Your 'Pennant Party' Perfect By Serving Cold Ortlieb's Beer." It made me feel very sad. I sat next to Mom, and we were silent for a long time. Finally, I spoke.

"Where do you think he went?"

She opened her eyes. "Probably to hunt down Chico Ruiz."

"Is Dad in the Mafia?"

"Oh, for heaven's sake," she said, collapsing back on the couch. There was another long silence.

"Do you want to hear an impression?"

"Yes. Do your LBJ."

I obliged with his hound-dog face, which got Mom smiling right away. Then came his drawn-out vowels.

"As we fiiight tha cooold waaar, ah say—Better Dead Than a Cincinnati Red!"

Mom laughed. "You have quite an imagination."

"I'm trying to write more jokes."

"Oh, you won't run out of material."

She pointed to the dining room table, where Taffy's ass was sticking out of her purse.

"That cat is the sanest one in the family," she said. "And he's licking a pocketbook."

We laughed.

I rested my head on her shoulder, and she kissed me on the forehead.

"Don't worry," she whispered. "They're going to win."

LITTLE LEAGUE

To my knowledge, there is no photograph of me in my 1964 Little League uniform. If there were, the team sponsor would surely produce waves of laughter from friends who have known me for decades as the polar opposite. But as I played the hot corner on the day before Father's Day, I had bigger things to ponder than words on a shirt—namely, the other team clearing the bases.

The lead runner rounded third and headed home.

"Hey, Lead Bottom!" he barked good-naturedly.

"Like to chat, but I gotta score," the second boy explained.

"My first home run!" the last guy shouted.

It was a picturesque day, sun drenched and graced by cotton clouds that hung on the horizon. The field had scuffed up foul lines and patches of worn grass, but from the pentagon plate to the cyclone fence, it was our little parcel of the national pastime. The bleachers were weighed down with a gaggle of locals: parents who clapped too much, an obese man who flicked cigar ashes off his tank top, clumps of chatterboxes who seemed less interested in the game than their fast-melting sno-cones.

Our coach walked to the mound and made a change. He took out Hapless and brought in Disaster. As the new pitcher warmed up, my friend Donny trotted over from short.

"We're getting the crap kicked out of us," he said.

"I know."

"But the Phils won two last night."

"Can you believe it? They're 14 games over .500!"

"You know, they get free beer in the clubhouse," Donny bubbled.

"Really?"

"Yeah. They can order anything. The fans don't get free stuff unless their program has the lucky number. I've never had the lucky number."

"My dad won a giant stuffed giant panda."

"At the game?"

"No. At my school."

Donny looked at the hill and shook his head.

"Disaster. He couldn't hit the nut sack on the Jolly Green Giant. Maybe you should pitch."

"I tried out, but I threw it into orbit."

"I thought you could hit a spot on your garage."

"That's the thing," I said. "My driveway goes up. I learned to pitch up. On a mound, I pitch *way up*."

Donny laughed. "You could hit Telstar!"

"Let's go!" the ump hollered.

The next play summed up our whole season. Disaster threw a hanging melon and the batter lined it my way. I froze, as it sliced into the outfield and past our leftfielder who was busy staring the other way.

My tendency to freeze was a problem, but the other kid available for third had run from a scorching grounder like a cat from a vacuum. With me, the coach had slightly better odds of avoiding extra-base hits, since some balls would just carom off my welted body and bounce back into the infield. The two double plays I "began" were scored "shin-6-3" and "groin-1-4-3."

Our time in the field seemed interminable. Cassius Clay could have knocked out Sonny Liston a dozen times. My Slinky could have slinked to Cinnaminson. As Disaster's ERA approached Friday's closing Dow, I scanned the stands, relieved that Mom and Dad were off running errands. An old guy pointed to the sponsor name on my shirt and gave me the "thumbs down." I looked away. At last, Donny caught a pop-up for out number three, and our fans hollered, "All right! Way to go!" Which might have been parental coddling for, "Life sucks! Get used to it!"

By the last inning, we were losing by some ridiculous score. I was up.

"Go Lead Bottom!" someone hollered from our bench.

Several of my teammates picked up the chant. "Lead Bottom! Lead Bottom!"

I had long since accepted this as friendly fun—from *them*. Trouble was, the kids on the other bench joined in mockingly.

"Lead Bottom! Lead Bottom!"

Their coach waved for them to stop. But good luck trying to muzzle the mischief of 11-year-olds who had been given bats and helmets and promised victory pizza.

"Lead Bottom! Lead Bottom!"

On an 0-2 count, I faced my usual dilemma. If I struck out, it was embarrassing. But if I got wood on the ball, it was even worse. I'd have to *run*. The pitcher, a gangly boy with Woody Woodpecker hair, got set. The chant grew louder.

What happened next was too damned unreal.

Woodpecker hit the outside corner with a fine fastball, and I swung and missed for strike three. But the ball bounced off the catcher's mitt and rolled toward the backstop, as my bench exploded: "Run! Run!"

I was paralyzed for an instant until it sunk in. The lesser of two evils had become the worst of both worlds.

"Go! Run!"

I stumbled out of the box, fixed on first. Down the line, I looked back. The catcher was lollygagging to the ball, showing me up. I

97

kept chugging. The first base coach waved furiously and shouted, "Come on!"

Head down, I told myself. *Keep moving!*

The ball flew past my ear, and I heard the enemy bench cheering. I looked at the first baseman, poised for the put out—*another* put out that would cement my rotten reputation. As the ball hit his glove, I pulled up. Then, unbelievably, it bounced out of his webbing and rolled toward Woodpecker.

"Run, run, run!" the first base coach exhorted.

My bench started jumping. Woodpecker scooped up the ball and decided against an underhanded throw; we were in a foot race to first. *Great*, I thought. *More running.* I plowed on, and my right foot crunched the bag a split second before Woodpecker's.

"SAFE!"

My teammates were all over it. "Lead Bottom! Lead Bottom!" The opposing coach waved over his catcher, most likely for a lecture on sportsmanship. I grinned. Next to the one game we won, it was the happiest moment of my brief baseball career.

After the game, we gathered around our coach.

"You guys hung in there and that was good," he said. "But we need to work on our hitting, pitching, fielding, and running."

Donny and I walked home along the White Horse Pike, on a beeline for sweets from the Oaklyn Bakery.

"That was one wild play," he said.

"Yeah. I can't wait to tell my folks!"

"Hey, what are you getting your pop for Father's Day?"

"Don't say 'pop.'"

"How come?"

"My aunt uses that word for dog poop."

"Pop? What's wrong with her?"

"Plenty."

"So, what are you getting your *dad*?"

"Anything but a tie," I said. "Every year I get him a tie. We're going to the mall today, and I'm getting something else. I swear it."

We sat on the sidewalk outside the bakery, stuffing our faces. A high schooler straggled by and stood above us.

"You guys are in for a rough year," he said.

"I got a double!" Donny shot back. "And he made it to first on a passed ball."

"No. I'm talking about your shirt."

We looked down and remembered our sponsor. In big letters, it read, "Oaklyn Republican Club."

He continued. "You're going to nominate *Goldwater*. If you'd gone with Scranton or Rockefeller, you might have had a chance. But now you're going to get clobbered."

Mom had scanned a list of teams and picked this one in a heartbeat. Maybe she thought we would play the "Oaklyn Commie Club." Maybe she had visions of a longhair caught in a rundown, as Donny and I taunted him:

"Balance the budget!"

"Free Cuba!"

"Stop experimental theater!"

"In your heart you know we're right!"

As the season wore on, maybe she expected Nixon to fly in for the final banquet and scold the other teams: "Just think what you'll be missing. You won't have the Oaklyn Republican Club to kick around anymore."

Then again, maybe she just wanted me to play ball and have fun.

The heckler moved on. Donny and I looked at each other and shrugged.

"What are you getting *your* dad?" I asked.

He thought for a moment and smiled. "A tie."

"No!" I screamed. "No ties!"

PHILS WIN!

National League Standings Morning of September 26, 1964				
TEAM	**WINS**	**LOSSES**	**PCT.**	**G.B.**
Philadelphia	90	65	.581	--
Cincinnati	88	66	.571	1.5
St. Louis	87	67	.565	2.5
San Francisco	86	68	.558	3.5
Milwaukee	80	73	.523	9
Pittsburgh	77	76	.503	12
Los Angeles	76	78	.494	13.5
Chicago	70	83	.458	19
Houston	64	91	.413	26
New York	51	102	.333	38

"Hi everybody, By Saam here. We're rolling along to the bottom of the ninth in an old-fashioned pitcher's duel between Art Mahaffey and Denny Lemaster. There's no score, but let's see if the Phils can get something going. Joining me in the booth, Rich Ashburn."

"Thanks, By. I'll tell you what—the Phillies *really* need a win. They've dumped five in a row, and the Cincinnati Reds are breathing down their necks. From Pottstown to Pennsauken, Phils fans are feeling the heat."

"Right you are, Rich. But nervous fans can take a Tasty break, with Tastykake. So much fun to put in your tummy, Tastykake cakes and pies! Well, it looks like Mauch is leading off the ninth with a pinch hitter. But *who's* coming out of the dugout?"

"Is that the bat boy?"

"No, Rich. I've just been handed some information from the front office, the place to call for tickets to tomorrow's game against these same Milwaukee Braves. Coming up is the team's newest bonus baby, from Haddon Township."

"Haddon what?"

"Township."

"Never heard of it."

"Relax, Rich. Try a Butterscotch Krimpet, made with farm-fresh eggs and creamery butter by the Tasty Baking Company, official sponsor of the Phillies, who play their final home game tomorrow with seats available, which can be yours by calling the ticket office at BAldwin 9-9200."

"What's the name of this kid?"

"Lead."

"Lead what?"

"Bottom."

"Never heard of him."

"Here's a cream-filled Koffee Kake."

"Thanks!"

"Right you are, Rich. Now, here's the skinny on Lead Bottom. He's eleven and a half, plays third, and isn't wearing a cup."

"Well, he's headed to the plate like a Quaker to a cathouse. Looks like he won't break any speed records."

"Evar Swanson holds the record for circling the bases. Did it in 13.3 seconds."

"What's Lead Bottom's time?"

"Tuesday through Thursday."

"Good one, By."

"Kind of you, Rich. Well, the fans sure are excited."

"LEAD BOTTOM! LEAD BOTTOM! LEAD BOTTOM!"

"Lead Bottom digs in. Lemaster looks in for the sign from Torre. Here's the pitch. Fastball. Swing and a miss! Lead Bottom not even close, as the crowd lets out a groan. The Braves pitcher not wasting any time as he leans in for another sign. Here's the 0-1 pitch. Swing and a miss! Lead Bottom really fooled on that change from Lemaster. But the fans are still with him. They're on their feet. To a man they're standing."

"LEAD BOTTOM! LEAD BOTTOM! LEAD BOTTOM!"

"Lemaster set for the 0-2 pitch."

"Hold on, By. Someone's hopped out of the stands."

"Yes, indeed. I'm getting some information from the front office where tickets are still available for tomorrow's finale."

"Looks like an *old woman*."

"Right you are, Rich. It's Lead Bottom's *grandmother*."

"Wow! And the fans love her!"

"NA-NA! NA-NA! NA-NA! NA-NA!"

"Nana waddles up to Lead Bottom. She plants a kiss on his cheek. And the crowd cheers! Now Nana turns to the mound. She walks to Lemaster with open arms. Lemaster steps off the rubber toward Nana. He has a big smile, too."

"By, I've never seen anything like it. The Braves are waving Phillies pennants! The Phillies are waving Braves pennants! The beer vendors are hugging the pretzel vendors! The ghost of Ty Cobb is kissing the ghost of the fan he beat senseless!"

"Lemaster leans down to embrace Nana. What a beautiful moment for baseball. Just listen to the crowd."

"KUMBAYA MY LORD, KUMBAYA. KUMBAYA MY LORD, KUMBAYA."

"Hold on, By. Nana is *not* letting go."

"Right you are, Rich. She seems to have latched onto Lemaster like a suckerfish. Good Lord! She's crushing him like a python! Lemaster waves for help. Here come the umps! Ed Vargo grabs her left leg. Shag Crawford grabs her right. They're trying to pull Nanaconda off Lemaster, but the old lady means business."

"I think Lemaster messed with her grandson, and she didn't like it. The house is going nuts! Both dugouts have emptied onto the field. And, whoa! There go Vargo and Crawford. She *mule kicks* them to the backstop!"

"Right-o, Rich. Now she *wrestles* Lemaster down to the mound, where it'll be Bunning and Cloninger tomorrow at 1:35 on the Phillies baseball network."

"The Phils and Braves are throwing haymakers! Lemaster and Nanaconda are somewhere at the bottom of a huge pile. Here come the cops! There must be 80 people on the field."

"The *perfect* time to send a special hello to 80-year-old Pinky Glans, a Phils fan who's in Hahnemann Hospital tonight."

"There's fighting in the stands! It's pandemonium! Giant stuffed giant pandemonium! The cops have dragged Nanaconda off Lemaster. He's completely out of breath."

"And so is Pinky, Rich. I received word from the front office that Pinky just passed."

"Sad."

"Yes, no more Tastykakes made from fresh eggs for him, but plenty of *goose* eggs on the scoreboard. It's nothing-nothing here in the ninth, as the umpires try to clear the field after a real donnybrook."

"Nana is led off to a standing ovation. She's the first grandmother these fans have cheered all year."

"Look, By! Here comes a *car* out of the Phillies bullpen."

"I'm getting details, Rich. That's Lead Bottom's *dad* driving. And in the back seat, it's *Bill Rohrer*, the mayor of Haddon—"

"Never heard of it."

"Wow! That car's a beauty, Rich. A '65 Caprice Custom Sedan with power steering, power windows, deluxe AM/FM pushbutton radio, tri-volume horn, and Quiet-Riding whitewall tires."

"In Nebraska, we'd call that a home for a family of 10."

"Good one, Rich. The Chevy stops at home plate, and Lead Bottom's dad opens the door for the mayor. He's a big man, a *great* man, a man of affordable financing for your next vehicle."

"The mayor sure knows how to make peace. He gives Lead Bottom a pat on the head and dishes out cigars for the umps. He snaps his fingers and here comes a ventilator for Lemaster. The Phils and Braves embrace!"

"Yesiree, Rich. This is the most beautiful moment for baseball since the one five minutes ago. The mayor gathers the umpires for a happy photo. He throws his arms around home plate boss Al Forman."

"Hmmmm."

"What is it, Rich?"

"I see through my binoculars that Lead Bottom's dad has slipped something into Forman's ball bag."

"What is it?"

"Can't tell yet."

"The mayor waves and gets back into the mist-blue Caprice. Lead Bottom's dad drives him off to another ovation. We're about set, as Lemaster sucks some oxygen and Lead Bottom steps in. Forman reaches into his bag and tosses a ball to Lemaster."

"Wait a minute, By. That's not a ball! That's not a ball at all!"

"What is it?"

"Forman just tossed Lemaster—"

"What?"

"An onion!"

"Right you are, Rich. And Lemaster doesn't have a clue. He's still in a daze. He rubs up the onion and gets set. Now, *Lead Bottom* sees the onion. He pounds the plate. His eyes are wild! Here's the 0-2 pitch. Swing and a long drive to deep left field! Carty going back ... back ... back! That putrid bulb is outta here!"

"Phils win! Phils win! Phils win!"

In 1964, I had plenty of baseball fantasies, many with Tastykake subplots, a salute to the pocket-sized Philadelphia classics we got from Nana's store.

On Saturday, as we followed the action on our family room TV, reality was a whole different ballgame. The Phils had chased Lemaster with four runs in the first two innings and clung to a 4-3 lead going into the final frame. Veteran reliever Bobby Shantz faced the heart of the Braves order.

Just three more outs, I thought.

The sunken family room was long, with pecan-colored paneling and a gray-and-white striped floor. One section was the television area. Facing the color set was a bargain rattan couch with vinyl-covered seating pads that always stuck to our summer-sweaty legs. Matching wing chairs, a wobbly rattan coffee table, and two Japanese wood-carved lamps completed another of Mom's Asian themes. The second section, near the patio doors, was our play area. It featured a speckled-blue, upright piano that had been pounded silly with "Chopsticks" (more of the Asian theme) and made to sound "cool" when Susan and I invaded its innards with a chain of paper clips.

Adorning the walls was Dad's sword collection: steel weapons from the Crusades, early American naval blades, and German daggers he shipped home during his push through Solingen and Munchen-Gladbach with the Ninth Army. "If the Russians attack," Mom said, "we'll be ready!" The closest we came to hunkering down, though, was at Christmastime, when Dad doused the lights so that he wouldn't have to tip carolers.

Mom and Dad had been icy with each other all day, and the

crack in The Great Happiness was the elephant in the room. *Just three more outs*, I thought. *Then we'll be back on track. Then I'll do my Mrs. Drysdale bit for a cheerful audience.*

Mom sat in a wing chair with her legs crossed: "One, two, three. How hard can that be?"

"Damn hard if it's Aaron, Mathews, and a pinch hitter," Dad growled as he fidgeted on the couch.

Taffy came running down the steps dragging Mom's purse. Lipstick, keys, and coupons flew everywhere.

"*That cat!*" Mom said.

Linda laughed. "He's looking for tartar sauce."

Susan and I laughed hard. Mom shooed Taffy and collected her things.

"Don't lose those coupons," Dad said. "And don't give him any fish. He has his own food."

The "one, two, three" scenario went down like the Hindenburg. Hank Aaron singled. Eddie Mathews singled. The two future Hall of Famers had set the table. Manager Bobby Bragan called on Frank Bolling to pinch-hit for Wade Blasingame. Blasingame was the *seventh* pitcher the Braves had used.

"They're playing like it's the damn World Series," Dad harrumphed.

"Everybody's after us," Mom agreed. "Like a pack of jackals."

Bolling smacked a grounder to Ruben Amaro at short. Amaro flipped it to Tony Taylor at second, and umpire Shag Crawford called Mathews out on the force. Suddenly, Crawford changed the call. *Safe!* Taylor had dropped the ball.

"What?" Dad hollered.

Mom covered her face. "What's *wrong* with us?"

"Freaking unreal," Linda said.

The bases were loaded, with nobody out. Rico Carty, an impressive rookie with a hefty average, was up. Shantz had handled him all year, but since Monday, it seemed the whole season had been turned on its head. Sure enough, Carty tore the cover off the ball. Aaron scored. Mathews scored. Bolling scored. Carty clapped his hands as he stood on third with a triple.

Dad had had it. He got up, set his glasses on the TV and trudged to the living room. The rest of us sat there stunned. Even Susan stopped playing with her plastic animals and blinked at the TV.

Somehow, we got to the bottom of the ninth down only 6-4. The Braves brought in their eighth pitcher. But it wasn't just any pitcher. It was the winningest lefty in major league history. He may have been in the twilight of his career, but Warren Spahn had already won nearly 350 games and had been a 20-game winner a record 13 times, including last year when he racked up 23 victories. I knew. I had read his biography.

Linda was livid. "They're mathematically eliminated, and they act like it's October. They're bringing in Spahn just to humiliate us!"

It was easy to think the deck was stacked against us. Or that Dad was right: We were cursed.

Years later I would find this game listed in the record books: The teams broke a major league mark for a nine-inning game by using 43 players, 25 Braves and 18 Phillies. But at the time, I simply remember my heart falling as Spahn set us down with ease. Any thoughts of doing Mrs. Drysdale also had been torpedoed. The last thing anyone wanted to hear was a skit whose punch line was, "Those Dreadful Phillies!"

We had lost six in a row.

"This is unbelievable," Linda said. "This is just unbelievable."

FATHER'S DAY

"Can you believe it?" Dad shook his head.

Mom covered her eyes. "I can't look."

We were in the family room, watching the first game of a doubleheader at Shea Stadium. As Jim Bunning walked to the mound to pitch the ninth, 32,000 New Yorkers stood and saluted him with yet another ovation.

"Listen to that!" Dad glowed. "Those are Mets fans cheering for *us*."

"He's loose," I said.

Dad nodded. "But you know he has butterflies the size of Texas."

"Why is everything the size of Texas?" Linda demanded.

Dad got out of his chair and turned up the TV. "All right. Here we go."

Mom folded her hands in prayer and squeezed them knuckle-white.

Nana clapped. "I hope he gets it!"

It was Father's Day, June 21, 1964. It was Dad's time, so I didn't point out that the date fell halfway between my birthday and half birthday. I only got a cupcake for my half birthday, so I figured a play for "quarter birthday" gifts would net me a swift kick in the pants. People put up with fractions only for so long. Besides, I already had my fondest wish: The Phillies had continued their torrid spring play and led the National League by one and a half games over the Giants.

Today, the baseball gods tantalized us. We were close to witnessing something that had not happened in 84 years.

It all began as our ace, Jim Bunning, stepped on the rubber to toil in the 90-degree heat. Catching the string-bean hurler was big Gus Triandos, who was Bunning's battery mate in Detroit. Bunning started strong, setting down Jim Hickman, Ron Hunt, and Ed Kranepool in the first. With a mix of pitches—an overpowering fastball here, a wicked slider there—he retired the side in order in the second, in the third, and in the fourth.

"Bunning's got a no-hitter," I said.

Linda rolled her eyes. It was not uncommon for me to mention a no-hitter after *one* inning, and my quixotic pronouncements had become a joke.

"He *is* sharp," Dad said.

"Didn't he pitch one with Detroit?" Mom asked.

"Yep," I answered, having memorized my 1964 Phillies Yearbook. "He no-hit the Red Sox in '58."

"I'm just glad we're winning" Dad said. "I don't know how long we can stick with the Giants."

I jumped onto the couch, between Mom and Linda. Dad and Nana occupied the wing chairs; Susan and Duchess sprawled on the floor. We were dressed up for an early dinner at Compton's Log Cabin Restaurant, which served first-class fare and was a welcome break from the paper-napkin eateries of the White Horse Pike. I was styling in tan slacks, buff short-sleeve shirt, and a striped clip-on tie, the coolest item in my bureau until 1968 when I got my first Hai Karate gift pack.

Bunning took a 2-0 lead into the fifth, got one out, and then faced catcher Jesse Gonder.

Gonder sent a shot into the hole between first and second,

but Tony Taylor stretched his body onto the outfield grass and smacked the ball to the ground. He grabbed it and pegged to first. Bunning retired the next batter and finished the inning with the no-hitter intact. In the sixth, the Phils offense kicked into high gear: Callison hit a solo homer, Triandos singled and knocked in a run, and Bunning helped himself with a double to score two. It was 6-0.

Bunning mastered the Mets in the bottom of the sixth and seemed to grow stronger with every pitch. His hard follow-through, which pulled him so far down that his glove hit the ground, seemed a relentless exclamation point to each bullet. Suddenly, everyone had joined me on the no-hitter bandwagon. By Saam mentioned that Bunning's wife, Mary, and one of his seven kids were rooting him on in the stands.

"Seven kids!" Dad howled. "Imagine his grocery bill!"

"Does he get paid a lot?" I asked.

"Oh, he makes plenty," Dad said. "Rick Wise is a rookie and pulls down seven grand a year. Bunning probably makes six times that!"

"How much do you make?"

"Not enough," Dad snapped. "I should be paid double for fixing other people's foul-ups. There's this one genius in the production department—"

"All right," Mom said. "Let's watch the game."

"I'm just saying, if you want something done right, *do it yourself.*"

This was one of Dad's oft-mentioned maxims, which had been whispered into his young ear, he swore, by none other than Thomas Alva Edison, one of America's great minds and control freaks. Dad had run into him at Philadelphia's sesquicentennial celebration in 1926, and the chance meeting took precedence, story-wise, over his glimpse of Patton (another control freak) during the war.

"What's he doing?" Dad would holler if Peanuts Lowrey screwed up a sign. "If *I* were in the box, we'd be up by 10 runs. If you want something done right, do it yourself."

"Maybe you could coach," I'd say.

"I don't have time to go down there. I have to put in the air-conditioners."

There was no such talk today. Even Dad was in awe of Bunning's control. During the seventh, he shifted in his chair. "I don't want to jinx it," he said, pausing long enough for Mom to jump in.

"No!"

"What?" Nana asked.

"What?" Susan echoed.

We sat mute, till I went for it.

"The *players* aren't supposed to talk about it, but we can," I told Nana. "He's pitching a perfect game."

"That's better than a no-hitter?" she asked.

"Of course!" Dad pounced. "No walks. No errors. No one reaches first. Twenty-seven up. Twenty-seven down."

"Good for him," Nana smiled. "Has he pitched one before?"

Dad looked at his mother as if she were daft. And with good reason. Since the National League was founded in 1876 and the American League began play in 1901, a pitcher had taken the mound to start a game 183,862 times. How many had pitched a perfect game? Only *six*. The historical odds of Bunning doing it today were roughly 30,000 to 1. The two perfect games in the National League both occurred in 1880.

"There's usually one or two no-hitters a year," Dad explained.

"Sandy Koufax no-hit *us* two weeks ago," I smiled.

Mom shot me a look.

I shrugged. "Sorry. Koufax is cool."

Dad went on. "But a perfect game? Forget it. You'll see a trustworthy politician before you see a perfect game."

"Everybody thought Eisenhower was on the up and up," Mom reminded us. "But he stole the nomination from Bob Taft—"

"All right," Dad said. "Let's watch the game."

As Bunning worked the seventh, we tried to joke about the

whole thing. But with each Met he sent packing, we grew more tense. Mom fussed with her hair. I started to count the swords on the wall. After the third out, we just collapsed. Dad got up.

"Everybody looks so serious," he said.

He smiled, stuck out his tush and let out a huge fart.

"Nooooooooooooooo!"

We cleared the room as Nana busted a gut.

Dad was onstage. "It's my day! I can do anything I want!"

We didn't even watch the Phillies bat in the eighth. Mom had opened windows to air out the room, and it was fairly fresh when we reassembled for Bunning's attempt to get batters 22 through 24. Linda brought down her transistor, so we had both the Phillies TV and radio coverage. Everything was set for big drama. Even the Mets fans were now cheering for Bunning, loud after he retired 22, louder after 23. Each at-bat was excruciating, and by the time Bob Taylor stepped in, we were a mess. Mom still had her hair, but I was counting and re-counting the outs on my hands like an obsessive-compulsive. Dad was literally on the edge of his seat and likely out of juice for another wind breaker.

Then there was more torture. Taylor worked the count full. This was it, I thought. If Bunning missed, it was all over.

"Over the plate," Linda whispered.

Bunning got set. He threw a slider and tried to catch the outside corner. Taylor took it. He spun toward first as if it were Ball Four, but home plate umpire Ed Sudol raised his arm. Strike Three!

"Oh my God!" Mom screamed.

I pumped my fist.

"Woo-hooooooooo!" Dad cheered. "Game of inches."

"*Millimeters!*" Linda breathed.

"Let's change the channel and see what else is on," Dad said.

We broke up. Eight perfect innings were in the books, and we chattered nervously.

"*Do you think the infielders want it hit to them?*"

"Thank God Taylor made that play in the fifth. Bunning should kiss him."

"Can you imagine what those ticket stubs will be worth?"

"It still stinks in here."

"Beans, beans, good for the heart. The more you eat, the more you fart!"

"Nana said, 'fart'!"

When Bunning came out for the bottom of the ninth, Shea Stadium was rocking. The 6' 3" right-hander from Southgate, Kentucky, had made only 77 pitches and struck out eight.

The announcers had already filled us in. The last perfect game was Yankee Don Larsen's gem in the 1956 World Series. The last regular-season perfect game was thrown by Charlie Robertson of the White Sox in 1922. The only National League perfect games were pitched in 1880 by Lee Richmond of Worcester and John "Monte" Ward of Providence. In 1959, Pittsburgh's Harvey Haddix lost his bid for a perfect game on an error in the thirteenth inning.

Dad got out of his chair and turned up the TV. "All right. Here we go."

Mom folded her hands in prayer and squeezed them knuckle-white.

Nana clapped. "I hope he gets it!"

Shortstop Charley Smith stepped in. Bunning got a quick strike on him. Smith took the second pitch high. Bunning fired another strike. Smith took a curve outside. On the 2-2 pitch, Smith sent a high pop fly into foul territory.

"It's playable!" Dad hollered.

Bobby Wine rushed over from short and made the catch.

We yelled and clapped and joined in the noise from Shea that poured from the radio and television.

"Two more to go!" Nana called out.

Bunning's powerful, sweeping sidearm delivery was a nightmare for right-handed batters. Left-handers hit him better, and

Mets manager Casey Stengel upped the ante by sending out George Altman to pinch-hit for Amado Samuel. Altman, a two-time All-Star with the Cubs in '61 and '62, was a solid threat.

"Work him tough," Dad told Bunning. "Stay ahead in the count."

Suddenly, I couldn't stop my leg from shaking. This was "fun" like the last few ticks of a climbing roller coaster. I pressed on my knee to steady it. So many things could go wrong. Bunning could lose control and plunk the hitter. One of our nervous infielders could boot a grounder. Altman could line one into the gap and ruin everything.

Altman went after the first pitch and lofted the ball to right. It was foul and Callison ran out of room as it landed in the stands. Bunning followed with a good breaking pitch in on him, and Altman fouled it off for strike two.

"That's it," Dad said. "Stay ahead."

Before I knew it, Bunning was dealing again. I pressed hard on my knee.

"Struck him out!" By Saam cried above the roar.

We whooped up a storm and tried to catch our breath. Dad turned up the TV again and Linda cranked up the radio. Volume, somehow, seemed our friend. Nana scooped up Susan and bounced her on her knee, "One more! One more! One more!"

Thirty-two thousand were on their feet, rooting for history. Stengel pinch-hit for the pitcher, sending out another lefty, John Stephenson, who happened to be from Bunning's home state. Two Kentuckians would decide it. My stomach was in knots and my leg was still shaking when Bunning delivered.

Swing and a miss!

The stadium roared. A chill went through me. I wondered how Stephenson felt hearing his own fans against him. Bunning threw again.

Strike two!

The noise was deafening. It was the loudest crowd I had ever heard. I had goose bumps. We all did.

"One pitch away!" Dad yelled over the din.

"This is it!" Linda said loudly in my ear.

The crowd kept screaming. Behind Bunning, the Phillies got into their fielding stances. The rest of his teammates were perched on the top dugout step. The great Ralph Kiner, now a New York broadcaster, was at field-level ready to interview Bunning.

Curve. JUST outside.

Sudol didn't give it to Bunning, and the crowd groaned and booed. We went limp like a family of rag dolls. The noise swelled again and lifted us back up.

Curve. Outside.

"This is maddening!" Linda said.

My leg was thrashing like a sack of cats. Mom took my hand and held it. I glanced around at the paneled walls, the rabbit ears on the TV, Mom's sunglasses on the squeaky rattan coffee table.

In this room, seven months before, we had mourned the loss of President Kennedy. Four years from now, we would gather again to watch Rev. Martin Luther King Jr.'s funeral procession in Atlanta and Ted Kennedy's emotional eulogy for his slain brother, Bobby. The next year, we would hang on Walter Cronkite's every breath as two Americans landed on the moon, and Dad would gush with pride and Mom would laugh that there had been no green cheese at all.

But on this day, Father's Day, Jim Bunning sailed a baseball to-ward home plate. John Stephenson swung—and our hearts stopped. He missed—and our hearts exploded!

"He gets it!" By Saam hollered.

We leaped from our seats and hugged. Yes! I clapped till it hurt. Yes!

"Can you believe it?" Dad said over and over. "Can you believe it?"

The Phillies mobbed Bunning, and the cheers went on and on. Horns honked down the street. Mom wiped away tears, and Nana had Susan in the Big Squeeze. The phone rang, and it was Aunt Nelle. "He sure ate his Wheaties today!" she told me.

After Bunning made it to the dugout, the New York fans continued to chant: "We want Bunning! We want Bunning!" He emerged to another ovation.

At Compton's, we feasted like kings. I imagined we were in a castle celebrating a great victory: Dad, the crown of Camelot; Mom, his fair bride; the rest of us, the hardened and happy warriors of a noble cause. The place was abuzz with talk of nothing else.

"Nobody pays attention to the Phillies," Dad told an excited waiter. "Well, the whole country is going to hear about us now."

That night his prediction came true. Jim Bunning made an appearance on Ed Sullivan.

At home, we caught the end of the second game, as Rick Wise won his major league debut, pitching eight solid innings and combining with reliever Johnny Klippstein on a three-hitter. The Phils increased their lead over the Giants to two games.

It had been one of the happiest days of my life. The only downer was that I felt a little crappy about my gift for Dad.

"I swore I was going to get you something better."

"Are you kidding?" Dad said. "I had the best Father's Day ever. I got two wins and a tie."

He grinned. His little play on words made me feel better.

Later, I realized how silly I was to believe that Thomas Alva Edison had really told him, "Son, if you want something done right, do it yourself." No. The Wizard of Menlo Park had leaned down to my father and whispered: "Kid, if you want to get a few laughs, stick out your butt and cut the cheese!"

AUNT NELLE

National League Standings Morning of September 27, 1964				
TEAM	WINS	LOSSES	PCT.	G.B.
Philadelphia	90	66	.577	--
Cincinnati	89	66	.574	.5
St. Louis	88	67	.568	1.5
San Francisco	86	68	.558	3
Milwaukee	81	73	.526	8
Pittsburgh	77	77	.500	12
Los Angeles	76	78	.494	13
Chicago	70	83	.458	18.5
Houston	64	91	.413	25.5
New York	51	103	.331	38

"Bunning better win today or we're in big trouble," Mark lamented. "But he's on two days' rest."

"He pitched in relief right before the perfect game," I countered as I pulled a white cotta over my black robe. "Maybe he'll pitch another one."

He quipped. "Where are the Mets when you need them?"

Organ music filled the vestibule of Our Savior Lutheran Church as we prepared for work. Our principal duties as acolytes were to light and extinguish altar candles and pass the offering plate. Or, as one kid put it, *flash, mash, and get the cash.*

I peered through the door crack, trying to spot wicks.

"How do they look?" Mark asked.

"Like crap."

There were three services on Sunday, and our family went to the middle one, which was a big bowl of misery for me. When the early-service acolytes put out candles, they purposely squashed the wicks, leaving us nothing but nubs. Then the miscreants hung around, falling all over themselves, as we struggled to re-light. Invariably, I panicked. The more I panicked, the longer it took. The longer it took, the more I felt the hot breath of worshipers, fed up with standing to sing, "Stand up, stand up for Jesus."

Our pastor, Floyd Paules, was a stout Pennsylvania Dutchman with an imposing nose and a flair for the comedic. He was purely Dickensian, from his tramp to the rostrum to his finger-in-the-air sermons laced with witty asides you'd expect to hear at a cocktail party.

"You think a minister's job is easy these days? I had to write a sermon yesterday with my kid's radio blaring, *'Come on, baby, light my fire,'*" he complained to laughs in 1967. He tagged it: "The *long* version."

He once offered a homily about a millionaire who died alone. Then, as the offering plate went around, he sneaked back to the podium: "I made up the whole thing. Dig deep!"

Today, Pastor Paules asked the congregation to pray for the Phillies.

I bowed my head and concentrated hard. I thought it was extremely important for us to out-pray the people of Cincinnati. Philadelphia had a bigger population, so that was a plus. But I figured our ace in the hole was something else. Philadelphia was the gateway to the enchanting Amish, and if God listened to anyone, it would be them. The Amish knew God's vocabulary. They wouldn't say, "God, please let the Phillies win the pennant." They'd say, "If it be thy will, let us ascend to glory. For thou art great."

But it begged the question: "Could we count on the Amish?" They had no TVs to watch the games, and I never saw them at Connie Mack Stadium. Did they even care about baseball? And what if a Reds fan came into Pennsylvania and turned the Amish against us? "Philadelphia was Ben Franklin's town," he would inform them. "And you know what *he* discovered. Electricity!" These scary thoughts were beyond my control. I would just have to trust the Amish to do the right thing.

After church, we were on our way to Harrisburg. It was a gray day with some light rain, and in the dense forests along the Pennsylvania Turnpike, the leaves had started to change. Fall was my favorite season, and I lost myself in the splashes of yellow that conjured happy thoughts of pumpkins and headless horsemen and brisk winds sweetened with the smell of chimney smoke. It was a quiet car ride; no one felt much like talking till we neared our exit.

"Aunt Nelle is going to be on the warpath about the Phillies," Mom warned.

"Is her picture tube still bad?" I asked.

"Damn," Dad said, remembering.

We parked in front of the brick apartments on Thomas Street and saw Aunt Nelle on the wet lawn. She stood with hands on hips, peevishly working a stick of gum.

"Told you," Mom said.

There was no mistaking Nelle Ulrich Seltzer.

She was of medium build with a slight paunch, but her pale skin held tight to her arms and hard face. The hair on her balding head was wild and white, feeding rumors that she had been a Hollywood double for Sam Jaffe, who played the Einstein-like doctor in *The Day the Earth Stood Still*. Her last known run-in with respectable grooming came in 1961, when her smiling mug made page one of the *New York Journal-American* after she won $11,000 in a Cash Word contest—a sum she spent on ocean voyages during which she was undoubtedly the talk of the high seas. The paper described her as "a sports-minded woman." She was half-deaf and spent less than a day fooling with hearing aids before tossing "the damn, worthless things" into a candy dish, where they were nearly eaten by her half-blind brother. She had a twitchy, playful mouth, which allowed her to star in the dual roles of blustery old broad and mischievous child. She was, in short, a character.

"Did you take the wrong exit?" she hollered, looking at her watch. "Or did you stop at Stuckey's for some pecan logs?"

"We made good time," Dad hollered back.

"No pecan logs?" she laughed. "Just as well for my constitution. Took half a bottle of Phillips to uncork the last one!"

Behind her, Aunt Vicki clutched a closed umbrella and waved. Aunt Vicki was Aunt Nelle's longtime companion and the sweetest lady I had ever known. They met in high school in Middletown, Pennsylvania, at the turn of the century, and after Grams's husband died in 1930, they moved into the big house in Pittsburgh to help out. Mom was their favorite.

"Oh, they never met any boys," Mom would tell us. "And if you weren't married by 23 or 24, you were considered an old maid."

Aunt Vicki had a round, Irish face and quiet manner. To those shocked by Aunt Nelle's testy tongue, she offered breathy apologies and freshly baked cookies. The two were as opposite as their check-marked favorites in the *TV Guide*: Nelle *"Wyatt Earp"* Seltzer and Victoria *"Lawrence Welk"* Kavanaugh. The only thing they seemed to have in common was a comical creeping waistline. Today, the band on Aunt Nelle's well-worn, cotton dress was bunched up around her midriff. Aunt Vicki's was headed straight for the boobs.

I was hardly out of the car before the self-proclaimed "Old Battle-Ax" yanked my ear.

"Well, what do you think of your Phillies and their tailspin?

The Whiz Kids pulled this stunt back in 1950 and nearly blew the pennant. It's always the same problem with that team. They need more coloreds."

"Negroes," Aunt Vicki tried to correct her.

"Allen is going places," Aunt Nelle yammered. "But the front office should have been signing the coloreds years ago. The Dodgers got Jackie early. No wonder they're world champions."

"What about Briggs and Johnson?" Dad said.

"Not enough," she barked. "We need more coloreds!"

"Let's go in," Mom said quickly. It was always dangerous to keep Aunt Nelle on a public sidewalk for very long.

Aunt Vicki whispered to Mom, "I keep telling her it's 'Negro.'"

Their second-floor flat was small—living room, kitchen, bathroom, and bedroom—and, as usual, Susan and I tore through it, inspecting everything. In the bathroom there was a rubber mat in the tub and some kind of girdle drying on the towel rack. In the bedroom there were framed portraits of Nelle and Vicki wearing smart suit jackets.

"This is when they were secretaries," I said. "They had to wear those get-ups."

At lunch in the crowded kitchen, Dad delivered a zesty recount of his "Chico Ruiz" moment.

"Well, isn't that a pip!" Aunt Nelle slapped the table.

"It sent them reeling," Dad insisted.

"Well, I don't doubt it, Hal. Something sure has put the whammy on them."

"Your grand nephew has been regaling us with funny voices," Mom smiled. "Ed Sullivan and LBJ."

"You pill!" Aunt Nelle looked me over. "Let's hear some good ones."

I was caught off-guard. I stared at my feet.

"Maybe later."

Mom gave me a hug. "After the Phillies win."

We had to watch the game on the temperamental black and white console. Dad fiddled with the set, and I grabbed the paper. I liked the Sunday sports section because it had the AP's "Major League Averages" for all players. Richie Allen was seventh in the NL in batting at .315, trailing only Roberto Clemente, Hank Aaron, Rico Carty, Billy Williams, Joe Torre, and Lou Brock.

"We've got two of the top five pitchers," I showed Aunt Nelle. "Chris Short is number two at 2.11 [ERA], and Bunning is number five at 2.38."

She snatched the paper. "And look who's *fourth from the bottom*. Ma-HEY-fey!"

Aunt Nelle had it in for Art Mahaffey, and I never knew why. He was a decent young pitcher who had a 12-9 mark, despite a sore arm. But she acted as if he'd swiped her Polident.

"He stood there and let Ruiz score! " Dad piled on.

"Trade him to the Cubs!" Aunt Nelle got going. "He'll have his fat offerings launched onto Waveland Avenue and sink that bunch from eighth to the cellar. The Cubbies haven't won a flag since '45 and surely won't win another if they continue to pull stunts like having their *coaches* take turns at the helm. That was the biggest circus act since Bill Veeck put up a midget. Too bad the little man didn't face Ma-HEY-fey—he'd have retired with a perfect average and a ticket to Cooperstown, where they'd have to put his plaque knee-high for other midgets. I keep writing the bigwigs at Shibe Park, who must have *midget brains*. Trade that Ma-HEY-fey to the Cubs, I say. And throw in old Swing-and-a-Miss Herrnstein!"

Susan brightened. "A midget played?"

"Eddie Gaedel," I said. "He came up once, before they outlawed it."

"Eddie Gaedel is right," Aunt Nelle patted my knee. "His number was 'one-eighth' and he batted for the St. Louis Browns. Cy Young himself couldn't hit that zone."

Dad kicked the TV.

"The picture takes a while," Aunt Vicki apologized.

"*Then* we'll see your folding Phillies," Aunt Nelle chuckled my way.

In the last few days, I'd noticed a subtle shift in her pronouns. The team was no longer "ours." It was "mine." Ma-HEY-fey, Fussy Gussy, Swing-and-a-Miss Herrnstein. I owned them lock, stock, and barrel. The picture faded in, and *my* Phillies took the field for the final home game of 1964.

Aunt Nelle squinted and pointed to someone she didn't recognize. "Is he colored?"

"No," Dad said.

"He looks colored to me."

"Your picture tube is going," Dad said loudly. "*Everything* looks dark."

She howled. "Oh, lordy. I thought it was an old Negro League game!"

"*Negro*," Aunt Vicki smiled thankfully.

"You remember them?" Aunt Nelle turned her way. "They sure were a bunch of talented coloreds."

Aunt Vicki shook her head and shuffled to the kitchen. It was no use trying to lasso the brain of someone who called Connie Mack Stadium "Shibe Park" and still referred to the Los Angeles Dodgers as "Brooklyn." Even though Aunt Nelle's terminology was out-of-date, she held every player to the same standard. He either delivered between the lines or incurred her wrath.

Felipe Alou started things with a grounder to Tony Taylor, whose running throw pulled Frank Thomas off first. Lee Maye chopped one over Allen's head for a two-bagger, putting runners on second and third.

"What's wrong with your Swiss cheese infield?" Aunt Nelle frowned at me.

Hank Aaron was fooled on a Bunning curve, but managed to get wood on the ball and loft it down the third-base line. It hit the chalk for a double and a 2-0 Braves lead.

"Oh, for crying out loud!" Dad said. "Here we go again."

"*Still* no breaks," Linda huffed.

"Right on the line," Dad railed. "We can't get a stinking inch?"

"The umpire was right on it," Mom sighed.

Aunt Nelle focused on the ump. "Is he colored?"

"No," Dad insisted. "You need a new TV!"

"I can't afford it! Old Johnson needs to put some extra money in my Social Security check. He's going to spend it all on Viet Nam. He should go over there and pick that Ho Chi Minh up by the ears and tell him to knock it off or deal with Goldwater, who will surely shove an H-bomb up his Red fanny. Yes, straighten out that Ho right now and bring our boys home. I can have some extra dough-re-mi on the first of each month and buy a color set so everybody looks jake. If this keeps up, I won't be able to tell Alvin Dark from Bill White. And, God knows, Dark is white and White is dark!"

Typically, there was a moment of astonishment after Aunt Nelle spoke. What could you say, really? Our discussion of a scratch double had suddenly been expanded to include Ho Chi Minh's anus. Aunt Vicki shuffled back from the kitchen with a platter of sliced fruitcake.

There seemed nothing wrong with the Phillies offense. In the first, Tony Gonzalez doubled and Allen singled him home. In the second, Clay Dalrymple doubled, Taylor tripled, and Bunning brought Taylor in on a sac fly. It was 3-2 Phils.

"Good for our boys!" Aunt Nelle clapped, with another slick transfer of team ownership.

But then came the fourth.

Joe Torre hit an easy grounder to short. *For some reason*, third baseman Richie Allen took the play away from Ruben Amaro; the ball caromed off Allen's glove for a single.

Rico Carty hit a perfect double-play ball. It took a *freak hop* over Tony Taylor for a single.

Denis Menke hit one to Amaro, who played it on the hop. *But it didn't hop.* Menke reached first as Torre scored to tie the game, 3-3.

Ty Cline doubled in Carty to make it 4-3 Braves.

The pitcher, Tony Cloninger, hit a pop fly. Outfielders Gonzalez and Covington thought Amaro would get it. Amaro *might* have gotten it, but *a gust of wind* blew the ball beyond his reach. Menke scored. 5-3 Braves.

Mauch lifted Bunning and brought in Dallas Green, a spot pitcher who had won 20 games over five seasons.

Felipe Alou greeted Green with a grounder. It *nicked the third base bag* for a double, as Cline scored. 6-3 Braves.

Lee Maye sent one past Green. Taylor nabbed it and threw home, but Cloninger slid in safely. 7-3 Braves. All seven runs were charged to Bunning. The Braves batted around and ended the frame with an 8-3 lead.

We sat, stunned. This even topped Aunt Nelle's seminar on nuclear proctology.

Dad stood up. "It's a curse!" Finding no room to pace, he sat back down.

"Three boners by the shortstop!" Aunt Nelle broadcast as she gulped the fruitcake and licked rum off her fingertips. "Amaro, Amaro—on the bench tomorrow."

"It wasn't his fault," Mom said. "Allen took one play from him and the wind took the other."

"The wind!" Linda steamed. "Who do we play tomorrow? The locusts?"

"I saw it all coming," Dad shook his head.

Mom rolled her eyes.

"The Braves are loose as a goose," Aunt Nelle said. "I told those pointy heads at Shibe Park to take the boys out for some sauce. The Braves probably have a case of Schlitz right in the dugout. They also have more coloreds."

"A *complete* mistake to pitch Bunning on two days' rest," Dad seethed.

"Bad hops and wind?" Mom countered. "How is that *his* fault? And if we're cursed, what does it matter *who* pitches?"

In the fifth, the Braves batted around again, pasting Green for four runs to make it 12-3. Dad left for a walk. Mom bundled up Susan for a trip to the playground just behind the apartments. Linda put her head on a pillow and dozed off.

"What do you think of your Dallas Green?" Aunt Nelle faced me. "A pinata doesn't get hit that much. Yes, a blind muchacho could knock him for a triple! How's your Spanish class? You should study hard and learn the language. I never had a knack for the foreign tongue, but I have a few choice words in plain English for the front office."

She sat at a desk near the TV, slipped a sheet into her old Royal and hit the return hard. She pecked away with both index fingers:

To the General Manager:

Green, Boozer, and Baldschun should be sent to the Cubs immediately. Get what you can for them and use the money to buy some decent relief. It is late September and there is no bullpen to speak of. I would come down there and pitch myself, but I am recovering from the gout. Poor Vicki has to do everything around here, but that is not your concern. If she didn't go to the market and keep house, I would send her to the Cubs. Ha. Ha. This 0-7 homestand is no laughing matter. Fire that bullpen and loosen up the boys as I've written you before or it's goodbye Phillies for 1964.

Nelle U. Seltzer

I walked into the bedroom to sulk. Why was this happening? Was the team pressing? Had Mauch messed up the rotation? Was Dad's foreboding *real*? Were we simply not good enough? Nobody had hard answers. During the broadcast, the camera had cut to a one-word sign hanging from the upper deck: "HELP!"

Aunt Vicki came in and sat next to me.

"Only five games left," I said glumly.

"Only five?"

I nodded.

"You love your baseball, don't you?"

"Sure."

"I remember Nelle back in high school. She went to all the games between Middletown and Highspire. Just couldn't get enough of it. In Pittsburgh, she'd sit in the bleachers at Forbes Field and yell her head off. Every year when the groundhog comes up, she starts talking about spring training and who's going to contend. She pulls the chair right up to the television and hollers for 'her boys.' Sometimes she gets angry and turns off the set, but five minutes later, she's right back, hanging on every pitch. And those letters she writes—half of them she doesn't even send."

I laughed.

"She'll be 80 next year. So, how many games do you think she's seen?"

"Thousands?"

"Probably thousands," Aunt Vicki agreed. "So, you see, there are a lot more than just five games left."

As we rode home, I thought about Aunt Vicki and what she had said. I smiled. I also felt good that our bats were still swinging; even though we lost, 14-8, Johnny Callison hit a home run in the sixth, another in the eighth and another in the ninth to increase his total to 31. However, I was concerned that the Amish hadn't done their part and prayed that they would start praying. The mood in the car was gloomy; it was a mausoleum on wheels. So, with her voice in my head, I attempted an impression of the Old Battle-Ax.

"Nobody listens to me about Viet Nam! Trade that Ho Chi Minh to the Cubs, I say! I'd kick his Red fanny to Wrigley myself, but I have the gout!"

There was instant laughter, and I kept going.

"I don't know what the gout is, but I have it. I got it from an old pecan log."

Everyone loved it.

"Old Johnson should send me some dough-re-mi for my good advice. I graduated sixth in my class."

This was a famous Aunt Nelle claim, and Mom played along: "You graduated sixth? Out of how many?"

"Seven!"

A little "Aunt Nelle" had flipped the entire mood, and I sat in the back of our Chevy puffed up like a peacock. I couldn't play the oboe or star in Little League. In fact, I had "no aptitude at all." But what began as a mimic of By Saam had led me to experiment with other voices, other characters. And now I had discovered the freakiest thing: I could make people laugh.

The car settled into a better silence, and I lost myself in the twilight. Only then did it hit me: The Phillies were no longer in first place. We had been atop the league since July 16, and for 73 magical days, I had never been happier.

"Second place" just didn't sound right.

FIREWORKS

"Whoever's in first place on July Fourth wins the pennant!" Dad proclaimed.

This was part of baseball lore, but also as accurate as the handed-down fiction that Abner Doubleday invented the game in Cooperstown. The '62 Giants won the pennant after being in second place on July Fourth. The '59 Dodgers, '57 Braves, and '56 Dodgers won the flag after being in *third* place on the hallowed day. But it was a dandy myth, and I was happy to embrace it, knowing the Phils would move into first with a win today over the Giants.

It had been a fine holiday, though more muted than our celebrations in Alexandria when Dad shot boxes of fireworks into the black sky, delighting onlookers up and down Myrtle Street. An errant rocket once slammed into old Mr. Grow's house, whereupon the codger had the good sense to hang out a white sheet of surrender.

Our first Fourth of July in New Jersey featured a debate about which pyrotechnics were legal and which would run us afoul of the local constabulary. In the end, we were given boxes of snakes and sparklers and instructed to tell disapprovers that Dad "knew the mayor." Susan and I dragged out the grill, and family friends Rosie and Isadore joined us for burgers crowned with bubbling Velveeta. What founding father wouldn't be thrilled to learn that

America was now the number-one consumer of processed cheese?

"Candlestick is a tough park," I answered Dad.

"Especially with that Giants line-up," Mom added.

San Francisco was one of the baseball's elite. They had won the '62 pennant after a three-game playoff against the Dodgers and took the Yankees the distance before losing a Game Seven heartbreaker, 1-0. Their offense was a powerhouse, boasting the league leaders in home runs for the past three seasons. In 1961, Orlando Cepeda, the "Baby Bull," took the crown with 46 homers (and led in RBIs with 142). In 1962, Willie Mays, arguably the greatest player of all time, belted 49 round-trippers. And in 1963, Willie McCovey tied Hank Aaron for the title with 44. Their mound brigade was anchored by the imposing Juan Marichal, who mowed down batters with a mix of pitches and who had won 25 games last year, tying Koufax for most in the majors.

A date at Candlestick Park (located on Candlestick Point, home to the plump candlestick bird) came with the threat of sudden fog, frigid temperatures, and swirling bay winds that reputedly could blow pitchers right off the hill.

Yesterday, the Phils kept their cleats in the terra firma and opened the three-game set with a 5-1 victory. Ray Culp notched an impressive win, scattering six hits through nine innings. Jim Bunning, whose perfect game was still fresh on the lips of broadcasters and admiring opponents, would go today.

The Phillies struck in the first when Callison walked and Allen delivered an RBI double off Jack Sanford. Bunning spotted the Giants two in the bottom of the first, and then settled in to pitch brilliantly. Sanford, who had won 40 games for the Giants the past two seasons, was lifted for a pinch hitter in the fifth when his hand went numb. In the sixth, the Phils tied it, 2-2. As the innings passed, the game took on the air of a fall-like classic: two heavyweights going toe-to-toe, the league summit on the line.

We kept one ear on the broadcast as life swirled about our

backyard patio on a faultless summer day. Rosie and Isadore had a raucous time and decided to rename Mom and Dad "Sylvia" and "Herman." Bruce Lazzery showed up with a pocketful of snakes, and we expressed our love of country by further desecrating the sidewalks. The Manuels arrived with red, white, and blue pastries, and there was a discussion about the versatility of icing. Grams called and asked if Ginger was still dating "The Catholic." By the time the phone was handed to me, she found it necessary, in her lathered state, to give me an eight-month heads up on my St. Patrick's Day wardrobe: "Don't wear green like everyone else. You should march into school wearing Protestant orange."

"I could use Quick Tan!"

"What? What is that?"

I panicked and hung up.

When the game moved to the eleventh, Mom, Dad, and I sat outside, lounging in the warm air. Duchess dealt badly with the distant booms and staccato of firecrackers along Heather Road. She despised this holiday. I figured all dogs would have been ecstatic had the British spanked General Washington and his ragtags. They would be quite content to loll under English rule, be served tea with their biscuits, and remain free from this yearly thunder that scared the pop out of them. Down the street there was a pitiful Chihuahua that trembled *as a matter of course*, and I supposed he was now rattling at the clip of a washing machine agitator, all because Cornwallis bollixed things at Yorktown. On the opposite coast, it was the Candlestick fans that shivered underneath blankets in the whipping winds.

"I can't believe they're wearing overcoats in the summer," Dad mused.

"Yeah, but what a game!" I said.

Reliever Gaylord Perry kept the Phillies in check. And Bunning had gone all 10 innings. He'd pitched scoreless ball since the first and retired 17 of the last 18.

"They have to get him some runs," Dad said.

"Herrnstein's leading off," I announced.

"Aunt Nelle's favorite," Mom laughed.

"Mahaffey's the one she doesn't like. Herrnstein's a close second."

"What does she call him?"

"'The Pop-up King.' Sometimes it's 'Pretty Boy.'"

"Sounds like a parrot."

"My grandfather bought a parrot that spoke Chinese," Dad said.

I did a double take. "Parrots can speak Chinese?"

"Yeah. He was out with the merchant marines and came back with this parrot as a gift for my grandmother. I'm telling you, she was mad as hell. She chased him out of the house with a broom and then tossed out the bird. *'I don't hear from you for two years and you show up with this blankety-blank parrot that doesn't even speak English!'*"

I laughed. "She really gave him 'the bird.'"

I laughed harder.

"All right," Mom said. "Watch your language."

Herrnstein halted his 0 for 14 slump with a blooper to right. Callison was up.

"Callison is much better looking than Herrnstein," Mom said. "I don't know what Aunt Nelle is talking about."

Dad chuckled. "Well, that's hardly her area of expertise."

I was confused. "What do you mean?"

Mom shot him a look and he clammed up.

"What?" I asked Mom.

"Never mind. Turn up the radio."

"It's up."

"Well then turn it down."

Callison fouled out. But Allen came through. He sent a shot to right center that the aging Duke Snider couldn't run down and sprinted for a triple, scoring Herrnstein.

"That Allen!" Dad exulted.

Our 6' 1" leftfielder, Wes Covington, was up. He had power, delivering 21 homers for the 1957 World Series champion Braves and boasting a slugging percentage of .662 in 1958. Almost as entertaining was his futzing around the plate: the step in, paw, dig, step out that drove Aunt Nelle bananas. *"The Old Slow-Poke!"*

"Old Slow-Poke" sent one over the right field wall. It was 5-2 Phils, and we loved it.

Mauch brought in Jack Baldschun to finish it off. Our bullpen ace, a master of five pitches, including the forkball, mowed down the locals, and it was "First place on July Fourth!"

Dad jumped up and launched into The Twist.

"Come on," I coaxed Mom.

She rose, laughing, and got into it. I scrambled to find some music on the radio.

"Keep going!"

I cranked up the Beach Boys and joined in the dance.

Round round get around,
I get around,
Yeah
Get around round round...

We segued from The Twist to a hula-hoop frenzy as Duchess ran for cover, now caught between gunfire and dancing Caucasians. The radio rang out Roy Orbison and The Shangri-Las, and soon there were glorious fireworks in the sky over Collingswood.

The night was filled with magic, and we clung to it like three happy fools.

The next day, Ruben Amaro drove in the winning run as Dennis Bennett bested Juan Marichal, 2-1. The Phils completed their first *ever* three-game sweep at Candlestick and moved ahead of the Giants by a game and a half. The pitching staff was dominant, holding Mays, McCovey, and Cepeda to a combined 4 for 33! Offensively, Richie Allen was no longer simply a rookie. He was a star. In the series, he went 7 for 11, with a home run, a triple, two doubles, and three singles, and his speed was a key factor in Saturday's win.

It was the All-Star break, and the Phils led the league with a 47-28 mark. When *no* Phillies were elected by the players to the National League starting lineup, we were stupefied. Dad was furious.

"They put Boyer at third instead of Allen? Allen's hitting 20 points higher!"

National League manager Walter Alston selected the pitching staff, and his seven picks included Bunning and Short. He also added Callison as a back-up outfielder. Mom was not mollified.

"Callison's the league MVP in a landslide. And he's a *back-up?*"

Dad wouldn't let go of the Allen slight. He rifled through the paper for ammunition.

"He's got 18 doubles, 16 home runs, and 47 RBIs. He's batting .308, and he's not an All-Star? It's a bunch of baloney."

I felt a kinship with Richie Allen, since we both played third base and were both offensive juggernauts. He ignited the Philadelphia Phillies, and I powered the Oaklyn Republican Club, where I ended my career just 2,997 hits shy of 3,000. I admired his power and determination. If he had occasional problems with the leather, so what? They don't call it the hot corner for nothing.

At the time, I didn't know the breadth of his struggle to make the majors. Dad had a clue, and that was one of the reasons he pulled for him. Allen grew up in Wampum, Pennsylvania, northwest of Pittsburgh, in abject poverty. His mother, Era, worked as a maid, with the harder, daily trial of keeping her children clothed, fed, and educated with little help from her estranged husband. The kids worked hard, the boys drew attention as forces of nature on the neighborhood hard courts and diamonds.

In 1963, Allen was the first African American to play for the

Arkansas Travelers, the Phillies' Triple-A club in Little Rock. He endured threats, racist taunts, and the humiliation of social segregation. He responded by leading the International League in home runs and RBIs, before being called up in September of '63.

Summer baseball in 1964 played out against an ugly backdrop: civil rights slayings in Mississippi and urban unrest in the North, including in Philadelphia. Before I was 11, I lived through the imminent threat of atomic annihilation and a presidential assassination. From Martin Luther King, Jr. and Pastor Beyer, I learned about the unfairness of segregation. This year, I heard enough snippets of adult conversation and watched enough Walter Cronkite to know what was going on. But I read the sports page more than page one, and was content to live in a happier world where my heroes were neither black nor white nor Hispanic, but just Phillies.

On Tuesday, July 7, the only injustices I focused on were that Richie Allen was not an All-Star and Callison would ride the pines.

As festivities got under way at Shea Stadium for the 35th All-Star Game, I sat in front of the family-room TV proudly sporting my Phillies cap and eager to spot our guys.

"Callison! Bunning! Short!" I punched my glove. "C-B-S!"

"Too bad the game's on NBC," Linda said.

"Dad says we're going to get three more channels."

"UHF," Mom nodded.

"Seven channels! How will we decide what to watch?"

"If you don't sit back from the TV," Mom said, "you'll be in no condition to see anything."

Linda rolled her eyes. "You can't get *radiation* from the TV."

"That's what the Russians want you to believe," Mom answered. "If they get enough of us sitting close to the TV, they won't have to drop any bombs."

I moved back. I was not about to be sent to my room and miss the All-Star Game, even if it were being telecast on a Cold War instrument of death.

"I don't know anything about the American League," Linda continued.

"Rocky Colavito is cool," I filled her in. "His real name is Rocco Domenico Colavito."

"Don't tell Grams," she laughed.

I looked at Mom. "Do I have to wear orange on St. Patrick's Day?"

"We'll talk about it later."

When the players were introduced, the trio from Philadelphia stood among baseball royalty. There were more colorful uniforms, with cardinals on a bat or an oriole adorning a cap, but nothing seemed so beautiful as those red pinstripes with "Phillies" stitched across the chest.

With a win tonight, the National League would pull even in the series for the first time at 17-17 with one tie. Nearly 51,000 were on hand to watch Dean Chance of the Angels go against Don Drysdale of the Dodgers. Bunning had been the probable starter, but he had worked those 10 innings on Saturday against the Giants. The AL lineup included three Yankees—Mickey Mantle, Bobby Richardson, and Elston Howard—and the night's only rookie, Tony Oliva of the Twins. The NL batting order was: Roberto Clemente, Dick Groat, Billy Williams, Willie Mays, Orlando Cepeda, Ken Boyer, Joe Torre, Ron Hunt, and Don Drysdale.

The AL slipped ahead in the first when Harmon Killebrew singled in Jim Fregosi. At the end of three, it remained 1-0.

"The announcer is good," I said.

Mom smiled. "Do you like that southern drawl?"

"Yeah."

It was Lindsey Nelson, the voice of the New York Mets. He was as smooth as By Saam, but more colorful, from his wild, plaid sports jacket to his jaunty play-by-play. He had started out in football, calling games for his alma mater, The University of Tennessee, and now complemented his baseball duties as mike man for the

Cotton Bowl on CBS. He would become my favorite sportscaster.

In the top of the fourth, when Lindsey Nelson announced that Jim Bunning was now pitching for the NL, I sat up and tightened my cap. Bunning stared in at Mickey Mantle.

"He knows a lot of these guys from his time with the Tigers," Mom said.

To thousands of baseball fans, Mantle was the embodiment of the sport and the Yankees were the gods of the game. If Bunning could handle them, as Koufax did in the '63 Series, there would be no doubt of his greatness. When our ace hurled his perfecto on Father's Day it was more dramatic, but this outing, it seemed to me, was more important.

"Popped him up!" Linda shouted even before Lindsey Nelson. Yes! We got into it.

"No easy outs," I exhaled as Harmon Killebrew stepped in.

The nickname "Killer" conjured up a bloodthirsty behemoth. But the Twins' outfielder was just 5' 11" and, by all reports, a kindly sort. It was his bat that was the killer; during the past five seasons he had averaged more than 42 homers a year. Killer greeted Bunning with his second single of the game.

"Rats," I said.

Bunning struck out the Twins' Bob Allison but gave up a single to the Orioles' Brooks Robinson, putting runners on first and second. Bobby Richardson, another Yankee, stepped in, and I buried my face in my glove, which was a primo place to hide. The Oaklyn ball field often featured nine little Republicans covering their faces with leather. Usually after a pop-up that no one wanted to field.

"Put down your glove and stop being silly," Mom said.

"I'm blocking the radiation."

"Don't be smart."

I lowered my glove and got to see Bunning strike out Richardson.

"Got both Yankees!" I yelled.

The crowd loved it, and Bunning walked off to an ovation. In the bottom of the fourth, Billy Williams hit one out to right and Ken Boyer parked one over the left field fence, and we celebrated the 2-1 lead with a second bowl of popcorn.

"Do they have popcorn in Russia?" I asked.

"If they do," Mom said, "they stole it from us. I read in the paper they're eating TV dinners now. Whatever we invent, they steal."

"Who invented the TV dinner?"

"The Swansons," she said emphatically.

"I'm glad we're not Russians," I said.

"Well, let's hope they don't take over. Let's hope we don't wake up one morning and find Yuri Gagarin on the Wheaties box."

She left for the powder room. I turned to Linda.

"Who's Yuri Gagarin?"

"I don't know."

"Mafia?" I asked.

"No!" Linda shook her head. "Maybe he plays for the American League."

I doubted it. Though during spring training I was convinced that our leftfielder was U Thant.

More important was that Bunning was now the pitcher of record. During a 1-2-3 fifth, he struck out Elston Howard, got Norm Siebern on a fly to center, and blew one past Jim Fregosi for a called third strike. In the bottom of the fifth, Alston pinch-hit for Bunning.

Mom sat up. "It's Callison!"

He popped up and Mom slumped back down. But Clemente singled and Groat doubled him in, as the NL took a 3-1 lead. In the sixth, Callison stayed in the game, playing right, and Chris Short replaced Bunning on the hill. It all looked good. Two Phillies were in the game, and if the lead held, Bunning would notch the win.

By the time Dad walked in, it all looked bad.

"Top of the ninth," I greeted him. "Americans ahead 4-3."

"I know. I heard on the radio."

He grabbed a seat and some potato chips.

"*Farrell* gave up the go-ahead run," Mom said, chiding the Houston pitcher. She grimaced as if he'd handed over Betty Crocker to the KGB.

Juan Marichal was now pitching for the NL. On Sunday we rooted against him, and now we were pulling for him. The dominating Dominican was on his game and got Colavito on a fly ball.

"Rocky got a double before," I smiled.

Mom frowned. I had expressed admiration for someone low on her pecking order, which today was (from worst to best):

1. Russians
2. American Leaguers
3. National Leaguers who give up go-ahead runs to American Leaguers
4. National Leaguers
5. Phillies
6. Johnny Callison

Marichal got the next two batters, and the game moved to the bottom of the ninth.

"Two runs to win," Linda announced.

"It's going to be tough against The Monster," Dad said.

The Creature from the Black Lagoon and the Phantom of the Opera held sway in my room, but the only big league "Monster" was Dick Radatz, the right-handed relief ace for the Boston Red Sox. Since his rookie year in 1962, the 6' 6", 235-pounder had decimated American League hitting with scorching, sidearm fastballs, prompting Yankees manager Ralph Houk to proclaim, "For two seasons, I've never seen a better pitcher."

The Monster had entered the game in the seventh, and his mastery of the last six batters included whiffs of Johnny Edwards,

Ron Hunt, Bill White, and Leo Cardenas. I found it unfair that the American League had The Killer *and* The Monster. Unless a mob of torch-wielding townsfolk arrived in Queens in the next five minutes, we were doomed. "Pitching is the name of the game," Dad always told me, and I knew there was nothing more intimidating than a hard-throwing reliever on a mission.

Willie Mays stepped in. In an instant he was behind in the count, 0-2. But he battled The Monster valiantly. He fouled off one pitch. And another. And another. And another. And another. He worked the count full.

"Hang in there," Dad coached him.

Radatz missed for Ball Four. We clapped. Mom and Dad inched up in their seats.

"Send him!" Dad implored Alston.

"The Monster's got a good move," I countered.

"*Have* to send him," Dad insisted.

"Mays can run," Linda said.

"He can *do everything*," Dad assured us.

Orlando Cepeda dug in. The Monster checked Mays and delivered.

"Swing and a miss!" Lindsey Nelson told us.

"He's holding Willie too tight," I said.

"*Gotta go*," Dad repeated.

The Monster dealt again.

"There he goes!" Dad and I shouted in unison.

Mays was off. Cepeda swung and missed, and Elston Howard fired to Bobby Richardson at second. There was a gigantic cloud of dust as Mays slid.

"Safe!" Lindsey Nelson cried.

"By a *mile!*" I hollered.

We had life. The tying run was in scoring position, and Mom and Dad inched up some more.

"That Alston is a good manager," Dad said.

Of course, had Alston not sent Mays, he would have been a bonehead.

"Now win it," Mom told Cepeda.

The Americans were shifted left, playing Cepeda to pull. Richardson held the fleet Mays close to the bag. Cepeda swung at the next pitch and placed it precisely where no one could get it—a bloop beyond first. The rightfielder was too deep, the first baseman too shallow, and Richardson, who might have been able to run it down, was minding Mays at second.

"In there!" Linda called it.

The crowd roared as Mays sprinted to third. He skidded past the bag in another eruption of dust and held up. Pepitone threw to the plate. The ball hit the ground and bounced high over Howard. Howard leaped for it, but the ball nicked his mitt and sailed to the backstop. The fans went wild.

"Go, go, go!" Dad shouted to Mays.

Willie took off and slid home in yet another blizzard of dust. Cepeda took second.

"Tied!"

We clapped hard, but Dad cut his excitement with caution: "The only thing more dangerous than a monster is a wounded one."

Radatz, indeed, proved his mettle. He popped up Ken Boyer. And after Johnny Edwards was walked to set up the double play, he fanned Hank Aaron on four pitches.

"No!" I slapped the floor.

The momentum had shifted back to the Boston prodigy. It seemed the best we could do was extra innings. Then Mom blurted, "Oh—oh!"

I looked at her and back at the TV.

"How about *this*?" Dad said.

We had forgotten the batting order.

The score was tied, 4-4, with two outs and two on in the bottom of the ninth. Lindsey Nelson's voice echoed the swell of the

Shea Stadium faithful. All their chips were placed on the next hitter.

It was Johnny Callison.

Mom folded her hands in prayer.

"Come on," Dad urged.

My glove was headed for my face, but I made a snap decision not to hide. It was a wise choice.

"Go, Johnny, go!"

Radatz delivered an inside fastball. Callison crushed it.

Mom and Dad were off their chairs in a flash. I scrambled to my feet and followed the ball as it sailed high over right field and into the seats.

"It's gone!" Dad shouted.

The crowd erupted. Callison circled the bases to thunderous cheers.

"On the first pitch!" Linda yelled over the volume.

"Can you believe it?" Dad said. "Can you believe it?"

We hopped up and down like kids on a trampoline as Callison was mobbed at home plate.

"Look at them!" Mom gushed. She clapped and leaned into the TV, radiation be damned.

The crowd continued to cheer. The stars of the National League met Callison with grins, hugs, and handshakes and jogged alongside as he ran off the field.

I wasn't even 12 and already I had my own version of Bobby Thompson's "Shot Heard 'Round the World" or Maz's 1960 curtain dropper. It was "The Swat that Slew the Monster."

When the *Bulletin* came out, Callison's blast was banner news. We passed it around.

"Listen to what *Koufax* said," I rushed. "'There's nobody in the league I would rather have hitting at a fastball pitcher like Radatz.'"

Dad grabbed the paper. "How about Dick Groat? 'There was no doubt in my mind that Callison would win the game for us. The Phillies can do no wrong.'"

I grabbed it back. "Listen to Ron Santo: 'The Phillies have it going. There's no stopping them!'"

I thought about it all day. We had the brightest young manager in the majors. Richie Allen was a rookie sensation. Jim Bunning hurled a perfect game on Father's Day. Johnny Callison won the All-Star Game with a dramatic, ninth-inning homer. We even had a triple play.

How could anything be any better?

CELESTIAL BODIES

National League Standings Morning of September 28, 1964				
TEAM	WINS	LOSSES	PCT.	G.B.
Cincinnati	91	66	.580	--
Philadelphia	90	67	.573	1
St. Louis	89	67	.571	1.5
San Francisco	86	70	.551	4.5
Milwaukee	82	73	.529	8
Pittsburgh	77	78	.497	13
Los Angeles	76	79	.490	14
Chicago	72	83	.465	18
Houston	65	91	.417	25.5
New York	51	105	.327	39.5

How could anything be any worse?

We had lost seven in a row, all at home. Freak plays, bad luck, nail-biters, blowouts, an extra-inning affair all added up to an unwelcome queasiness deep in the gut. Meanwhile, the Cincinnati Reds, who swept a doubleheader from the Mets on Sunday, were on fire. They had won nine in a row, and as Mom surmised, seemed intent on winning it for Fred Hutchinson, who was battling cancer and had taken leave as manager on August 13. Even the Cards were back in it. A week ago, we were going to the World Series. Now it was a three-team dogfight, with our snake-bitten squad headed in the wrong direction.

After the Phils were dumped into second place, Mauch put a brave face on it: "Maybe we're better going after something than holding onto it."

I wanted a break from the whole mess and tried to focus on *anything else* during the mile-long walk to school. Sometimes I'd take the quiet way, down Heather Road to Lees Lane and around the lake, where ducks preened and an occasional oddball stood fishing for eels or other wretched creek fare. Today, in the drizzle, I opted for the noisier route: up Heather Road to heavily traveled Cuthbert Boulevard and a straight, downhill shot to my destination. I arrived at the back of the sprawling, sand-colored brick building, slipped through a football field gate and headed to the place where I would spend the next six years.

"Haddon Township is an excellent school," Dad told us after we moved. "It has the best teachers in South Jersey."

Of course, Dad could bring home a $10 electric fry pan from Korvette's and convince us it was the secret tool of the great chefs of Paris. This time, though, Dad was near the mark. I ended up with a solid education, high SAT scores, and an easy path to college.

I loved Spanish, English, journalism, history, and math. In tenth grade, I spent happy hours doing geometry proofs and balancing chemistry equations; the logic and order of it thrilled me. I tolerated art (finagled Mom into drawing my homework), music (still no aptitude), health (went to sleep during a discussion of "calcium" and never woke up) and gym (hell itself, run by little men with whistles).

By the grace of God, the summer sobriquet, Lead Bottom, did not follow me to the gymnasium. My athletic embarrassment did. As I went down in a wrestling match, arms flailing, the class laughed uproariously. Mark Ritter (from church) informed me that my shorts were on backwards and the HTHS hawk was planted squarely on my ass. Gym was a disaster from the first days of seventh grade. We were called one by one for our physicals, but my name was never uttered. An investigation determined that I had been placed on the girls' list as "Carol Wolfsohn."

About this time, I realized I had a troublesome *last* name. It was the "h" in it that threw everybody. Roster readers were totally flummoxed.

"Carl Wolf—"

There would be a pause.

"Wolf—"

Another pause.

"Wolf-SHON?"

Only my music teacher, Claire de Krafft, got it right.

"It's like Felix Mendelssohn," she smiled. "Sohn is the German spelling of son."

Meanwhile, I was Wolf-SHON, Wolf-SONE or worse. The "h" would terrify writers as well; in a panic, they would dump it anywhere: Wohlfson, Wholfson, once even Hwolfson.

Over the years, I have saved prescription labels, dry cleaning receipts, etc. with various misspellings of my name. I have been identified as Walfson, Welfsohn, Wholfshn, Wolston, Wolfjohn, Wilofson, Wilson, Wolfsblan, Wolfoohin, Wolfshen, Wolfsen, Wolson, Wolfeson, Wolfsoln, Wolfsohan, Wolffon, Wolfsonn, Wolfsomn, Wolfston, Wolfnson, Wolhsolm, Wolpon, Wolpohn, Woolfson and Woltoon.

My favorite was printed on a hotel bill. Carl Wikfsihn.

It didn't take me long to realize this was the product of a sloppy typist who hit "i" for "o" and "k" for "l." But for several weeks I mulled over changing my name to Wikfsihn, fancying myself a shadowy double agent from the eastern bloc. On a dank, Bucharest side street, I would light a cigarette and whisper to my contact, "I am Wikfsihn."

He, a fat fellow in a fedora, would convulse with laughter.

"Wikfsihn!" He would laugh some more. "You are not Wikf-sihn! You are Wolf-SHON. And your funny, capitalist underpants are on backwards!"

The murdering of my name made me determined to be a precise speller when regarding classmates or teachers. *Lester Schaevitz. Jeff Kowalczyk. Mr. Vandegrift.* On the flip side, I realized how the misspelling or mispronunciation of my name (disorder) could get some laughs. In this new arena of more than a thousand kids and instructors, I was already scouring the halls and blackboards and cafeteria for any kernel of comedy. If I could do an impression of Aunt Nelle, I could certainly imitate Mildred Joy as she coaxed us to trill the Spanish double *r*.

"Man's best friend is a *perrrrrrrrrrrrrro*."

She would show us her tongue in a disturbing way, while spraying the front row.

"A *perrrrrrrrrrrrrrrro*."

I had never seen a Spanish dog, but I imagined it to be buried under a mound of human slobber. (*"Senor, que clase de perrrrrrrrrrrro es ese?" "Es un spitz!"*)

On the way to homeroom, I passed two teachers huddled in the hall. They were talking about what was all over the radio: After a ten-month investigation, the Warren Commission concluded that Lee Oswald acted alone in assassinating the president. The two were not convinced.

"It was Castro!"

"It was the Mafia!"

Mafia? I walked straight into a locker and nearly broke my face.

I entered Room 241 and sat at my desk, next to Frank Zampino. He was a swell guy, quiet but funny, and a budding artist whose cartoons kept me in stitches. Lately, he had been drawing our homeroom and square-headed math teacher, Mr. Kerns. These caricatures were presented to me during quiet class time and kept coming till

I burst out laughing, which would nettle the unsuspecting victim himself. I would see his square-headed wife and try to suppress a laugh. I would see his square-headed dog and let out a few snorts. I would see his square-headed dick and lose it.

Zamp looked up and gave me a nod.

"Everybody's talking about who shot Kennedy," I said.

"I'll bet your mother thinks it was the Russians."

"You know it," I laughed. "If the car won't start, she thinks Khrushchev's been in the garage."

He grinned. Then he shook his head. "The question isn't who killed Kennedy. It's who killed the Phillies."

The mess was back in my head. And at home, the *Evening Bulletin* had more bleak news.

"Big Magic says our odds of winning it are just 16 percent," I told Mom.

She was on the couch, deep into a book, and didn't hear me.

"What are you reading?"

"Oh," she looked up. "I found this book on astrology at the mall."

"What's astrology?"

"It's the study of celestial bodies and how they affect people."

"Celestial bodies?"

"The sun, the moon, the planets. Astrologers chart their movement to see how they influence us."

I didn't get it.

"You know Wolf Man up in your room?" she asked.

"Yeah."

"When does he act up?"

"When the moon is full."

"There you go. The *moon* influences him."

Two hours later, she was still absorbed, as Dad muttered at the sports section. He lit up.

"Did you see what Bob Oldis said? Right here in Sandy Grady's column."

He read it: "The whole mess seemed to start with Chico Ruiz' steal of home that beat Art Mahaffey. I've never seen anything like that run of breaks."

He waved the paper.

"My premonition was right!"

"Could be," Mom said. "The most psychic signs are the water signs—Cancer, Scorpio, and Pisces—and you're a Cancer. But Callison is a Pisces, and *he* didn't have a premonition. Look at Ray Kelly's story."

She got up, took the paper and read: "Callison, during last week's plane ride back from Los Angeles, refused to take the pennant for granted. He said: 'We've got to keep bearing down. We haven't won this thing yet.' John confessed *it was not a premonition*. Only that some teammates 'were spending the World Series money a little too soon.'"

She handed back the paper.

"Of course, Cancer and Pisces are just sun signs. There are planetary influences that could determine who's psychic. It's all very complicated."

Dad stared at her. "What are you talking about?"

"Astrology," she answered. "If an astrologer did the team's horoscope, he might realize that the Phillies are being negatively affected by celestial bodies."

"Wait!" I shouted. "I just remembered. The night we were at the game was a full moon."

Mom jumped in. "That's right. It was."

I was excited. "So Chico Ruiz *was acting crazy* when he stole home. Maybe he's The Wolf Man!"

Dad looked at me and looked back at Mom. "You're both nuts."

We gave him a pointed look.

"Okay," he gave in. "We're all nuts."

At 7:30 we watched *Voyage to the Bottom of the Sea*, and I was pretty shook up by the sinister agent who released "fear gas" on the Seaview. The series would become one of my favorites, as Admiral Nelson and Captain Crane battled pissed-off plankton, Lobster Man, and the ghost of Moby Dick.

Voyage had some excellent writing and special effects, but in the end, it was as silly as Zorro out-dueling an army of swordsmen. The admiral and captain sailed through episodes entitled "Doomsday," "The Edge of Doom," "Deadly Waters," "Deadly Invasion," "Deadly Cloud," "Deadly Amphibians," "Deadly Creature Below," "Cave of the Dead," "The Deadliest Game," "The Death Ship," "The Death Watch," "The Death Clock," "Death from the Past," "Fires of Death," "No Escape from Death" and "A Time to Die"… and somehow managed to live. By the tenth grade, part of me wanted to see an episode called "The Delightful Dolphin," where the entire crew got wiped out.

I went to my room to listen to the game. The Phils were at Sportsman's Park in St. Louis to take on the streaking Cardinals, who had won five in a row. After logging a 39-40 record before the break, Johnny Keane's Redbirds had gone 50-27 thereafter, behind the bats of Lou Brock, Curt Flood, Bill White, Ken Boyer, Dick Groat, and Tim McCarver (all hovering around .300) and the arms of Ray Sadecki, Curt Simmons, and tonight's starter, Bob Gibson (all near 20 wins). Gibson had an overpowering fastball, curve, and slider, which he could place anywhere he pleased. Mauch tabbed Chris Short to stop the Phillies' skid, even though the lefty would have to work for the fourth time in 11 days. Dad's reaction was hardly understated.

"Damn! Where's Wise? Where the heck is Culp? He hasn't started in a month."

In the second, the Phils got two men on but came up empty. Short surrendered two singles and a run on a sac fly. In the fourth, Gibson retired the Phils 1-2-3. Short got nicked for a double, a single, and a run on a fielder's choice. In the sixth, Gibson was flawless, but Short didn't have his good fastball. Boyer doubled and White singled him in. It was 3-0 Cards, and Mauch gave Short the hook. Short later admitted to having some pain in his left forearm, but swore he wasn't tired.

"We need runs!" I pounded the bed.

I was restless and walked into the hall. Linda's door was closed; Mom was in the living room. I heard laughter on TV and figured Dad was in the family room watching some late-night show. Taffy brushed by me with little compassion for the state of things. I headed into the master bedroom, where I often snooped around. Once, I smelled nicotine in the bath and found of pack of Kents hidden under the sink; another time, I spotted Mom taking a drag as she stared out the bathroom window. On a rare occasion in Alexandria, Mom would light up a Kent, or Dad would smoke a pack of Chesterfields, but, basically, we were a vice-free household, unless you consider wearing fashion from J.C. Penney to be a bad habit.

For a spy like me, Dad's bureau and the heap of clutter next to it was a treasure trove. Buried in one drawer, I had already discovered a novelty lighter. It was a naked woman imaginatively labeled "My Old Flame." When you flicked it, fire would shoot out the tits.

Taffy sat in the doorway, and I told him to keep watch as I picked through Dad's floor pile. There were shoes, shoe polish, broken pencils, folders, a paperback copy of *The Power of Positive Thinking*, and scraps of paper with scribbled reminders. "Check oil." "Invite Hunters to dinner." "Relax!" I opened a folded sheet of paper, torn from a yellow legal pad, and it stopped me. It was the outline of a letter to Mayor Rohrer:

Bill,

What a year for the Phillies! I know you'll have many requests for tickets, but I'd be grateful for a chance to see a game.

My son would never forget his old man taking him to a World Series.

I stared at it for a long time. Even at a young age, I could hear the pathos when Dad spoke the words, "my son." There was a heaviness he carried about never knowing his father.

Finally, I folded the paper.

"We're going to *win this game*," I told Taffy.

With one out in the eighth, the Phillies responded. Gonzalez walked and Allen singled to center, putting runners on the corners. Callison hit one to third; Boyer made the play at second as Gonzalez came home on the fielder's choice. It was 3-1, with Covington up and Callison on first. A long ball would tie it.

I rocked. "Come on. Come on."

It didn't take long. Covington smashed the first pitch to deep left center.

"Get out!"

It flew 400 feet...

"Get out!"

...but Curt Flood snared it, just short of the wall.

Just short.

That close.

Almost.

Another heartbreak.

The Cardinals showed no mercy in the bottom of the eighth, tacking on two more; the Phillies helped with an error and a wild pitch. In the ninth, the crowd of 24,000 gave Gibson a standing ovation. I sat on my bed feeling helpless. Mom came in quietly with the laundry basket.

"Are you all right, honey?"

"Yes."

She managed a smile and put some socks in my drawer.

"Let's get to bed," she whispered. "You have school tomorrow."

As she left, I could see she was crying.

For a long time, I couldn't sleep. The house was silent, except for a few coughs from Linda's room. I tossed. I stared up at the top bed. I thought about Dad's note and the World Series tickets that were already printed and what the players must be thinking and why Covington's ball couldn't have gone a few feet farther. It was worse than summer music school, but I was determined not to cry. What would my friends say if they saw me crying?

But then, there was the absurdity of it all: Dad had a premonition that Chico Ruiz, who was really The Wolf Man, would ruin our season, which, according to Mom, might have already been doomed by celestial bodies. God could intervene, of course, but that would only happen if the Amish started praying.

That was enough to start me laughing. For a while, at least.

It was so funny it hurt.

BOY SCOUT COOKIES

Throughout the summer of 1964, from the dramatic All-Star Game on, my nose was happily planted in the pages of our daily. Its slogan was, "In Philadelphia, Nearly Everybody Reads *The Bulletin*." I was a bit offended that the tag line excluded us. It wouldn't have killed them to slap up a billboard: "In the Heather Glen Section of Haddon Township (Oaklyn ZIP Code), Nearly Everybody Reads *The Bulletin*."

It was an afternoon paper and perfect for us, since mornings were chaos. I had to fight my sisters for bathroom time. Breakfast was a free-for-all. Duchess had to be walked. Taffy was let out to do his business, which he conducted in the next-door sandbox. This exercise in free enterprise sent Harriet and Chuckie Olson squealing to their mother, who called Mom, who lectured Taffy. Of course, you do not lecture a cat. The Olson kids were condemned to retch and run as Taffy watched with seeming delight from Susan's bedroom window. Dad told Mom the Olsons should "get a dog or be grateful their kids learned at an early age that life is full of crap."

There was plenty of life's crap in the paper—war and hatred—but I skipped over most of it and devoured the fun stuff. In the August 2 *Sunday Bulletin*, there were spectacular photos of the moon taken by Ranger 7. There was a story about the opening of the Beatles' first movie, *A Hard Day's Night*, which noted the Fab Four's upcoming Philadelphia concert where "utter teen-time pandemonium" was expected. In sports, there was a picture of Mets manager Casey Stengel celebrating his 74th birthday by lapping a gigantic lollipop. The story added:

"He is a natural born comedian, but behind his clownishness is a brain second to none. On and off, Stengel has been managing baseball teams since 1926. How much longer he will continue is problematical. He shrugs off talk of the future with this retort: 'Most men my age are dead by now.'"

I laughed and plunged into coverage of yesterday's game at 21st and Lehigh. Jim Bunning was touched up for four runs in two innings, but his Dodger counterpart fared worse. Don Drysdale was shellacked for seven runs in three innings, as the first-place Phillies prevailed, 10-6. Rick Wise, in middle relief, picked up his second win; both Tony Gonzalez and John Herrnstein went 3 for 5. It was our 60th victory, putting us 19 games over .500.

Tonight, John Boozer would get a rare start. When the lineups were announced, Linda pointed out that our eighth and ninth hitters were "Wine" and "Boozer." I toasted them with a tumbler of grape Fizzies.

Chief Bender aside, most baseballers "of the spirits" had crashed and burned: Clarence Beers pitched one game for the 1948 Cardinals, gave up four runs in less than an inning, and retired with an ERA of 13.50.

Tinsley Ginn had a single at-bat for the 1914 Cleveland Naps and exited with a .000 average.

Ernie Lush played one game for the 1910 Cardinals and went hitless.

But Bobby Wine was our stalwart shortstop whose .971 fielding percentage earned him a Gold Glove in 1963. And Boozer was a tall righty who battled wildness, but managed three wins last season and a decent ERA of 2.93. So, in retrospect, we should have been proud that Wine and Boozer had already out-performed Beers, Ginn, and Lush.

By now the high-flying Phillies were national news. *Sports Illustrated* did a spread on them, and *The Saturday Evening Post* ran a feature on Gene Mauch with the headline, "The Whip Who Put the Snap in the Phils." And I couldn't wait to scoop up our own paper to read my favorite beat writers: Ray Kelly, who reported on the games, and Sandy Grady, who penned a "Man About Sports" column.

Kelly packed his stories with all the ballpark drama, and his feature leads were playful:

"Rain today—and the forecast of more tonight—brought the Phillies some relief from the plague of lefties."

Grady gave me the lowdown I couldn't get from the back of a Topps card:

"It is apocryphal that if Gene Mauch should sneeze at midnight, 3,000 miles away, Clay Dalrymple would stir in his sleep and mutter, 'Gesundheit!' It is true, though, that Dalrymple, this blocky, balding ex-fighter, has been molded into Mauch's alter ego, an uncanny extension of the manager's mind…

"…Without a catcher operating on the same wavelength, a manager is as dull as an unplugged computer. Only the Phillies pitchers know how Dalrymple has become the cerebral cortex of this club, instantly flicking the right decision—i.e., Mauch's—to the nerve ends…

"Before they began doing a mental tango on the same beat, Dalrymple and Mauch went through years of sweat, mistakes, cussing and warfare. Dalrymple puts his feet up on the empty clubhouse table and talks about it with the same grudging grin marines wear discussing their Parris Island drill instructor."

These scribes had a wry sense about them, and I ate it up. I also found myself looking up beaucoup words in Webster's. If something about the Phillies was "apocryphal," I had to be clued in. It was apocryphal that George Washington threw a dollar across the Potomac. On the other hand, there is some evidence that the beefy

William Howard Taft got stuck in the White House bathtub.

My love affair with the sports page was interrupted during the second week in August. Boy Scout summer camp fell during the exact time of our family vacation, and I had to choose between the two. Considering that I had been in only six states, a trip to Maine sounded unbeatable. But my first summer camp at nearby Pine Hill held the promise of midnight ghost stories and woodsy camaraderie.

"You awaken to an exciting new day with your best friends," my Scout handbook assured me. "You look out through the open tent door and see a smiling sun in a blue sky—then jump out of bed, grab soap and towel, and join the others for the morning wash. The cook sounds off: 'Come and get it!' Not a moment too soon! What a breakfast! Hurry now—there's the call for swim!"

"Lunch everybody! The patrol cooks of the day are doing themselves proud!"

"Campfire!"

"Happy dreams!"

I was again seduced by exclamation points and delved into the camping section.

"There are four kinds of poisonous snakes in North America," I told Susan. "The rattlesnake, copperhead, coral snake, and water moccasin."

"Can a snake get in your sleeping bag?"

"No!"

"What if you get sick?"

"I won't get sick."

Linda chimed in. "You're due for sixth disease."

They cracked up.

"That's so funny I forgot to laugh."

Dad scanned the list of required supplies and scrounged up as many items as possible, including his World War II canteen and a broken pocketknife.

"It says I need a compass."

"Ginger had one. You can use hers."

"It's a Girl Scout compass!"

"It's fine. It points north."

"But it's a *Girl Scout* compass!"

"Ever heard of a Girl Scout lost in the woods?"

"No."

"See. Theirs work better."

I taped over the Girl Scout insignia, terrified of being fingered a Brownie or Camp Fire Girl. It was bad enough that I had to dress in olive shorts, gartered knee socks, and a zipped kerchief and be bullied by one neighborhood kid as a "Swiss Fruitcake."

The first day was pretty cool, except for the lake. We were divided into three groups: non-swimmer, beginner, and swimmer. A round tag attached to our trunks identified us: blank for non-swimmers, red for beginners, red and blue for swimmers. I didn't have championship form like Dad, but I *could* swim. If worse came to worst, I could save myself with a furious doggie paddle. But I identified myself as a non-swimmer because there was no way I was jumping into a lake full of the things I feared most—snakes. I decided it was wiser to be mocked as a non-swimmer than reveal my ophidiophobia to a pack of pranksters who might fill my tent with fanged serpents. So I endured two hours of toe dipping with the sallow blank-taggers who marked time with the talk of the damned.

"You're not supposed to go in until an hour after you eat."

"That's why you'll never go in, FAT ASS!"

"Shut up!"

"You shut up. You have bigger tits than my sister!"

"Hey! Where's my lotion?"

"Check your butt hole, albino."

Just as promised. *You awaken to an exciting new day with your best friends...*

My tent mate was a slight, happy boy named Rusty Daisy, who laughed as I checked and re-checked my sleeping bag for stray reptiles. On the first night, we heard rustling outside. I froze. Had some kid brought a rattle and shook it around our tent, I would have bit it right there.

But then we heard giggling, and poking through the tent flap came a non-poisonous pink trouser snake. The 1964 Phallus Festival was under way, and within minutes we were dashing through the brush to see "what Dieter can do with his!" Dieter's was the first uncircumcised penis I had ever seen, and I stared at it like it was the star offering of a freak show. For a while I believed one kid's explanation that Dieter got his member stuck in an electric pencil sharpener.

Someone must have ripped every other chapter out of the handbook. Pine Hill was hikes, dicks, swimming, dicks, whittling, dicks. *Come and get it!*

When I could break away from The Festival, I clicked on my transistor, a lifeline to By Saam, Bill Campbell, and Richie Ashburn. In Maine, they were scanning the airwaves, too. My first letter from Mom, dated "10 August 1964" (she still used the military dating style from her time at the War Department) mentioned baseball right away:

"Heard the Phillies won Sat. and Sun. Did you hear the games? Hope they keep winning. We're sort of isolated here, but the radio comes in handy. We get a Canadian station, and they rotate programs in English, French, Spanish and Italian. We hear the ball scores at the end of the day, and coming up we heard the Red Sox-Chicago game on the radio. We miss you lots. Here's an extra dollar, but don't spend it all on candy."

I didn't. I spent it on a bribe.

For newcomers, the most feared part of camp was "The Initiation." I was told it could occur at any moment in any number of forms. The past tortures were related with such transparent hyperbole that I laughed—until I heard about the kid who was staked out while the gang unbagged a snake on him. I was already half nuts scouring my bunk at bedtime; *this* I didn't need. When one loudmouth whispered to me that he could "fix it" so I wouldn't be initiated (remember, this was New Jersey), I coughed up Mom's Washington without delay.

Within hours, I was naked.

I was lathered with shaving cream and assorted jellies and marched before the whole, howling troop (the scoutmaster and assistant scoutmaster "took a walk" during initiations). I tried to smile. But then loudmouth sprinted from my tent.

"Look!" he hollered. "He's got a *Girl Scout* compass!"

It was passed around, along with the ripped-off tape.

"He tried to hide it!"

It was *Lord of the Flies*. Even the blank-taggers joined in the savage chants.

"Girl Scout! Girl Scout!"

(Never a good day when you long for "Lead Bottom.")

"Sell us some cookies."

"Yeah. We want cookies!"

At the moment, the only "cookies" within reach were hanging between my legs. And it did occur to me that if I could vend them for 50 cents each, I could make back my wasted bribe. As loudmouth led the catcalls, I came to a cross conclusion: The idea that all Boy Scouts were "trustworthy and loyal" was a bunch of bunk. In fact, it was downright apocryphal.

Rusty got a similar stripping and left for home immediately. I stuck it out. Despite the night of humiliation, I had some fun at Pine Hill and learned lifelong skills. To this day, I keep a safe distance from groin-level pencil sharpeners.

At home, the Manuels dropped off our *Bulletins*, and I plowed through a week's worth of sports sections. The Phillies had won seven of eight! In one inning against the Mets they sent 12 men to the plate and scored eight runs in a victory keyed by Callison, Covington, and Amaro. The next day, Bunning fired a shutout and lowered his ERA to 2.23. The Phils breezed into The Windy City and took two of three from Chicago. "CALLISON HITS GRAND SLAM AGAINST CUBS," trumpeted Tuesday's front-page headline. Veteran first baseman Frank Thomas, who was picked up on waivers from the Mets, banged out three doubles in the 13-5 rout. "PHILLIES WIN 6-5; COVINGTON HITS 3-RUN HOMER," shouted Wednesday's front page. Clutch play by rookie Johnny Briggs earned him some good ink from Kelly and Grady. Grady wrote:

"Briggs is the good luck charm, a magic amulet around the Phils' neck, deadly against evil spirits. A losing game? Like a gambler flowing on the dice, Gene Mauch calls on Briggs, whose base hit is a signal for the Phils to rumble. It happened again yesterday—and never mind that diving three-run liner which he played as smoothly as a bear doing the frug in a pair of snowshoes."

The next series at Shea Stadium opened with a Friday twi-night doubleheader, and Mauch trotted out his lucky Father's Day duo of Bunning and Wise. Bunning went the distance, scattering five hits, and Thomas vexed his former mates with two RBIs, as the Phillies won, 6-1. Allen logged three hits in the nightcap to help Wise earn the sweep, 6-4. Saturday, the Phils hammered the hapless Mets again, with Boozer notching the 8-1 laugher.

I held up the August 8 paper to Dad. "Look! In Houston, they're building a stadium with a *dome*. It's air-conditioned."

"Can you believe it?" he said, checking out the photo. "Says it'll seat 46,000! You could get lost in a place that big."

I went upstairs and tossed the compass on his stack of stuff. Just in case he needed it.

After returning from Pine Hill, I realized how much I had missed baseball. "Happy dreams" were not promises in a handbook. They were the daily rhythms delivered to us on WFIL, and the smiles of a summer night as we took a solid lead into the ninth.

During an eight-game home stand beginning on August 17, the Phils took two out of three from the Cubs and four out of five from the Pirates, outscoring their opponents 46 to 18. Three words started to appear in print: "The World Series." Danny Cater, who had been on the DL with a fractured wrist, was about to be re-activated. "I just hope I can get off the disabled list in time," he said. "In time for what?" he was asked. "In time for the World Series. You have to be on the roster by September 1st." In a photo below the story, Cater was all smiles as Frank Thomas and trainer Joe Liscio played tic-tac-toe on his cast.

Whatever lineup Mauch scratched onto the scorecard, it came up roses. If the pitching faltered, the offense took up the slack. At Pittsburgh on August 29, Mahaffey and Boozer gave up *eight* runs in the final two innings, but Allen and Callison had already salted away the 10-8 win with seven RBIs. By September, we were 27 games over .500 and led the Reds by 5 1/2 games and the Giants by 6 1/2.

Winning was infectious. I danced about my room and started to call the games with a nifty impression of By Saam.

My new friend, Sandy Grady, had the spirit, too. In an August column, he reported from the team plane:

"The difference between traveling with a winner and a loser is simple. One is a chore, like battling the expressway traffic to a job you don't like. The other is euphoria, a picnic to which you invite Mamie Van Doren, blue skies, and no ants."

Seven paragraphs later, however, there was this:

"'Sure they'll win it,' [Richie] Ashburn said. 'The only thing that could stop them would be a big collapse. They depend enormously on Mauch, though. I don't know how that will work out when the pressure comes.'"

PLEASE, MR. POSTMAN

| | | National League Standings | | |
| | | Morning of September 29, 1964 | | |
TEAM	WINS	LOSSES	PCT.	G.B.
Cincinnati	91	66	.580	--
St. Louis	90	67	.573	1
Philadelphia	90	68	.570	1.5
San Francisco	86	70	.551	4.5
Milwaukee	82	73	.529	8
Pittsburgh	77	78	.497	13
Los Angeles	77	79	.494	13.5
Chicago	72	84	.462	18.5
Houston	65	91	.417	25.5
New York	51	105	.327	39.5

Ray Kelly's lead summed it up.

"*St. Louis, Sept. 29—The Phillies, engulfed in the worst collapse in major league history, are third placers today with dimming hopes of winning the National League pennant.*"

I sat cross-legged on the living room floor scouring the sports section; Mom sat on the couch with front-page problems.

"Now, *China* may test the bomb."

"We still have a chance," I said.

"Goldwater won't take any guff from them."

"It's Bennett tonight."

"Plus, Johnson is a Virgo. Much too feminine to deal with the likes of Mao."

"He can even his record at 13 and 13."

Mom put down the paper. "13 and 13? Sounds like a Libra."

I wasn't aware that Dennis Bennett *was* born on October 5 and *was* a Libra; much more concerning was his lifetime record of 1-6 against the Cards.

The phone rang, and Mom was soon engaged with The Old Battle-Ax. Dad walked in from work, and I felt like making mischief.

"Who's on the phone?"

"Mom."

"I know *Mom's* on the phone. Who's she—?"

"She's upset because China has the bomb."

"Who is she talking to?"

"Could be Meow Say Tongue. What are the rates to China?"

"China!"

"For heaven's sake!" Mom called out. "I'm on with Aunt Nelle."

Dad peppered me. "Who called? Did she call or did Aunt Nelle call?"

"Aunt Nelle called."

Dad was relieved that his wallet wasn't being drained.

"But Mom may have called her back."

"What? She called her back?"

"Good lord!" Mom said. "She called *me*. Calm down." She pointed at the Chinese symbols. "Peace!"

"That's happiness!" Dad countered.

Mom rolled her eyes.

"Happiness," Dad confirmed to me.

"Bennett's going tonight."

"Oh, man," Dad exhaled. "Everyone at work is sick about it. I can't even read the paper."

Mom held up the receiver and motioned me over.

"Callison has the flu. Aunt Nelle heard it on the radio."

Dad collapsed. "What *else* can go wrong?"

Taffy ran by him with a fish fillet.

Dad put his head in his hands.

"Aunt Nelle?" I began.

"What a bust! Why does Mauch pitch Short when his arm is a rubber band? And now Callison has the shakes. I blame the front office. They should have been scouting the streets last month when the coloreds were rioting. Could have found a few pitching arms among those bottle throwers or some good batsmen among the boys in blue.

"Old Gussie Busch cleaned out his front office in August, and now look at the Redbirds—only a game out. I told Vicki that my letters must have ended up in St. Louis instead of Philadelphia. Heaven knows where any of the mail goes these days with that new ZIP code.

"I have to hang up because this is costing me small fortune, which I should bill to those Einsteins at 21st and Lehigh."

"Okay."

"Do your homework and mind your parents."

"Okay. Bye."

No one spoke much during dinner. Mom didn't seem to care that I didn't touch my vegetables. I asked to be excused and Dad nodded.

As the slide continued, we were no longer listening to the games as a family. And I was at the point of accepting my power-lessness. I had prayed, hoped, dreamed, changed my routine, and not produced a single win. Time was running out. I had one last play to call, but it would depend on the speediness of the U.S. Postal Service and the actions of two important grownups.

As the pre-game played on my radio and Taffy watched from

the windowsill, I tore two sheets from my spiral notebook, sat at my desk and penned the letters. I read the first one to Taffy.

Dear Commissioner Frick,

How are you? I hope you and Mrs. Frick are fine. I am fine. I know you care about baseball fans like me.
Everybody is really upset that baseball got switched from 154 games to 162 games. So I think you should proclaim that the season was OVER on September 24. How great would that be? Like old times!

Your friend,
Carl Wolfsohn
Third Base

Taffy remained unconvinced.

"Well, not everybody is upset about the long season. But lots of people are."

I scanned my feline conscience.

"All right. It's a fib. But I'm sending it anyway."

I folded the last-ditch appeal, slipped it into an envelope, added the baseball office address that I copied from my *1964 World Almanac and Book of Facts* and affixed a nickel stamp.

The game was under way, so I set aside the second letter and settled in. The pennant that Dad bought me at the ballpark eight days before—"Phillies National League Champions 1964"—hung on my closet door, and I wished it a talisman as the Phils batted in the first.

It was Ray Sadecki, going for his 20th win, who had the magic; he set us down in order, to the satisfaction of 27,000 fans clearly buoyed by the surging Cardinals.

As Dennis Bennett warmed up, I sought reassurance from my Phillies yearbook that boasted of the 6' 4" lefty from California,

"With Bennett challenging batters like a seasoned veteran, fighting back in the toughest of situations, the Phillies look exceedingly strong on the mound."

All the wishful words evaporated in an inning and a third as Bennett was drubbed for five hits and three runs.

The yearbook offered fancy talk on every player.

Dazzling speed. Poise beyond his years. All the tools for greatness!

According to that, the Phillies should have wrapped up the pennant in April. The mischievous part of me wanted Aunt Nelle's club manual.

Third Base Coach George Myatt—The old goat has blown more signs than a liquored-up Helen Keller.

We were down three runs early, but I was determined not to give up. Not giving up had replaced wishing for a win. Sadecki had a streak of 20 straight shutout innings when the Phils finally got to him in the fourth. He walked Allen, Phillips, and Amaro. Mauch pinch-hit against the lefty with right-hander Gus Triandos, who smashed a single to center, scoring two.

After five innings, down only 3-2 in a hostile park, I felt jaunty and ran downstairs with my envelope.

"I wrote a letter to Commissioner Frick!" I told Dad.

"What?"

"We're getting runners on," Mom offered from the couch. "We just need a long ball to take the lead. If only Callison weren't sick!"

"What's this letter?" Dad asked.

"I told the Commissioner he should call the season over at 154 games. Like it used to be."

Mom laughed. "I'd go for that."

"I also wrote to—"

"It's a nice thought," Dad interrupted. "But you used a stamp for *that*?"

"You never know," Mom said. "He might read it."

"That's *five cents*," Dad protested.

"Oh, for heaven's sake," Mom said.

"Five cents is five cents."

They were off.

"Well, if you'd let me *call* my mother instead of *writing* her," Mom pressed him, "we'd have more stamps."

Yikes! Grams was now involved.

"Writing is cheaper than long distance," Dad said.

"I do write. But when can I *talk* to her?"

"When she has something useful to say!"

"You're as stubborn as she is," Mom told Dad. "And she's a Taurus."

"I have no idea what that means. All I know is *nobody* likes her. Roosevelt was going to declare war on her or the Japanese, and Hirohito won on a coin toss."

"Good thing *you* weren't there. You wouldn't have given him the coin."

"That's right. I'd save it."

"Mother said you were cheap."

"So, she *did* say I was cheap! When did she say it?"

Wow, I thought. I could have reported that to Dad, made a nickel and paid for my own stamp.

"You should call her and ask," Mom said.

Dad threw up his hands.

"It's a sweet idea," Mom told me. "Give me the letter and I'll mail it tomorrow."

"Perfect," Dad said, pointing to the envelope. "He put a Shakespeare stamp on it. This *whole thing* is a tragedy."

"Shakespeare also wrote comedies," Mom argued.

"He wrote tragedies. *Hamlet* was a tragedy."

"*Much Ado About Nothing* was a comedy."

"Nobody saw it. That's why he called it that."

I fled before Peace vs. Happiness broke out.

In the sixth, Bill White's towering drive into the right-center bleachers made it 4-2 Cards. It was off John Boozer, the fourth of *six* Phillies pitchers that would be used. Our seven pinch hitters included Frank Thomas whose broken thumb was still in a cast. Mauch was throwing in everything he had.

In the seventh, that included Callison.

Weak and shaky, he walked to the box and singled to right. The batboy ran out with a jacket, usually allowed only for on-base pitchers to keep their arms warm. Callison couldn't even button it. First baseman Bill White did it for him.

Sandy Grady captured it the next day:

"Even the Cards watched Callison's grim trudge to the plate with admiration... They trotted out a red jacket to Callison at first base, but he was too chilled and jittery to button it.

"'I had to fasten his jacket for him,' said St Louis' Bill White. 'You gotta hand it to a guy like that. Maybe it sounds ridiculous, but I think everybody in this clubhouse feels sorry for the Phils...'

"But gallantry wasn't enough... They came up empty against the antique knuckleballer, Barney Schultz...

"Mayo Smith, who managed the club before he became a Yankee scout, watched them filing dolefully through the Chase Hotel lobby. He had seen much of the Phils' swan dive compiling a World Series report he can doubtless stick in the waste basket.

"'If I hadn't seen it, I wouldn't believe it,' Smith said. 'No club in history ever got so many bad breaks with a pennant in its hands. You'll never see this again.'"

It was late. I was slumped in my desk chair. Mom pushed the door open and offered her salve for our ninth straight loss.

"Callison tried. They're all trying. And we still have a mathematical chance."

I stood up and she hugged me. I was determined not to give up and not to cry, but I was on the verge of tears. Suddenly, Mom pulled way. Her eyes were wild, and I followed them to the second letter on my desk.

"What!" she said loudly.

Dad walked in.

"What?"

She picked up my message and read it aloud.

"Dear President Johnson, How are you? I hope you are fine."

"He's not fine!" Mom admonished me. "And neither is the country."

"Oh, God," Dad moaned.

Mom continued reading.

"I wrote to Commissioner Frick and asked him to end the season after 154 games. If you call and tell him to do this, I think you will win a lot of votes in Philadelphia and New Jersey."

She raised her voice as Taffy scampered from the room.

"Maybe even my mother will vote for you."

"Uh oh," Dad said.

I stepped back.

"I would *never* vote for that crude Texan. Didn't you see him in April picking his dogs up by the ears? Who does that? Would you torture Duchess? And I hear he cavorts *naked* in the White House swimming pool! That's just vulgar."

I cringed.

"At least Roosevelt used the pool for therapy and wore trunks. Can you imagine Ike swimming nude? Never."

Mom had just demanded that I contemplate President Eisenhower's bare ass. Someone had to stop her before Mamie's tits came up.

"I was just thinking about the Phillies!" I said.

"You never know," Dad jumped in. "Johnson might read it."

Mom recoiled. "How can he stop baseball when he can't stop the Communists? At least Goldwater will stop the Communists."

"Goldwater is losing votes because he wants to stop Social Security," Dad said.

"He *didn't* say he would end Social Security. He said contributions could be *voluntary*."

"That might end it," Dad countered.

"Whose side are you on?" Mom raised her voice.

Crap. This was the moment it might get ugly. I thought quickly.

"Aunt Nelle would get mad if she didn't get her Social Security. Can you imagine her letters?" I channeled her. "To the Social Security front office: Who's in charge down there, and where's my money? Who's sending out the mail, Old Slow-Poke Covington? I might just send Pretty Boy Herrnstein to sweet-talk your secretaries into action. I need some cash by Friday to do something with my hair since Vicki now says I look like one of those Beatles who are surely all on *dope*."

It worked.

"*Exactly* what she would say!" Dad said.

Mom laughed.

"Can I send the letter?" I asked.

"I think it's great!" Dad said. He pulled out his wallet, took out a stamp and gave it to me.

"If you're putting a stamp on that," Mom said, "I'm going to call Mother!"

Dad trailed her out of the room. "How long? No more than 10 minutes!"

I felt really good. I probably stopped a major fight and turned it back into bickering, which was, quite simply, much ado about nothing.

If the Phillies were finished and there would be no World Series, there was another diversion tugging at my heart. Comedy was all around me. And I had found it.

BASEBALL IN BLACK AND WHITE

"John Wilkes Booth rode through here after he shot Lincoln," Aunt Elsie told me.

"Really?"

"Yes! He stopped at a doctor's house a few miles from Waldorf to have his broken leg set. Then he hid in the woods."

"They caught him, though."

"In Virginia."

"He was bad. Just like Oswald."

"Bad men," she agreed. "Crime doesn't pay. And neither do these one-armed bandits!"

Elsie put a final nickel into the slot machine, pulled the handle and came up unlucky again. I glanced outside the market at Grams, who was sitting in Elsie's light blue Ford Falcon.

"Grams won't come in?"

Elsie laughed. "Oh, no. She doesn't approve."

Two days before Labor Day 1964, I added gambling to the list of things that irked Grams.

"Yes, gambling has been going on in Charles County since the late '40s!" Elsie bubbled like a tour guide as she zipped along in the Falcon. "This whole area was known as 'Little Las Vegas.' The paper says there are still more than 2,000 slots."

"Not in the churches!" Grams interrupted.

"Of course not," Elsie said.

"Sin city," Grams clucked as she shook her head.

"When we get home, you can help Jimmy with the stone work," Elsie told me.

"Cool!"

That spring, Aunt Elsie, Uncle Jimmy, and Grams moved from outside D.C. to sparsely populated southern Maryland, halfway between the former tobacco market towns of Waldorf and La Plata. Jimmy bought five acres off Route 301 on which he built a long, ranch-style home with an artful field stone exterior. He spent three years on the project, on nights and weekends, and it was the ultimate monument to the self-made man who had run away from his Indiana farm at 15, rode the rails to the Pacific Northwest, labored at odd jobs, served in World War II, and ended up in the U.S. Coast Guard teaching electronics at Fort Belvoir, Virginia.

Like Connie Mack Stadium and Boy Scout camp, "the country" was a captivating flight from suburbia, and Linda, Susan, and I each got our own summer week there.

I helped carry groceries into the kitchen, where Grams peered into the bags for Papist Pillsbury products. I sprinted out back, into the warm air flavored by distant wood smoke and livened by a chorus of cicadas.

"Can I help?" I called to Jimmy.

"I think so!"

He was working on the last section of house exterior, smoothing mortar under a large, beige stone he had set in place in the grand mosaic. He handed me the trowel.

"Give it another swipe."

I carefully evened out the mortar.

"Good," he said.

Jimmy gathered more mortar from a wheelbarrow, lopped it in place, and pointed to a smaller stone in the pile.

"Let's try that one."

I placed it, Jimmy adjusted it, and I smoothed the mortar again. This was like a puzzle, and high art at that. I loved it! Jimmy knew just the right stones he wanted, by color and shape, and it was a rush seeing how it all came together. We worked for the next hour, building.

Jimmy was a man of few words, which I always regarded as wisdom gathered from a life of adventure.

"Aunt Elsie played the slots, but she didn't win."

"Well, that's the way it usually ends up."

"You don't play?"

"No. If I pay good money, I like to know what I'm getting in return."

"Grams says it's a sin."

"Not sure about the sin. Just don't like the odds. I figure if I got out of the war alive, that was enough good luck for me."

"The Phillies are lucky this year!"

"Looks like it."

"The World Series is next month."

"I hope they make it."

"They will," I pronounced.

"I'm not much for baseball," Jimmy said. "And the Senators, well…"

"They are bad," I said.

The Washington Senators were an expansion team in 1961, after the previous Senators took off for Minnesota and became the Twins. This year's squad was in the midst of a seven-game losing streak, which included four consecutive shutouts. On this day, they stood at 53-85, 30 games behind the White Sox. I felt bad for their manager, Gil Hodges, who had been an eight-time All-Star for the Dodgers and stood up for Jackie Robinson. Five years later, though, Hodges would craft the greatest managerial feat in MLB history with his Miracle Mets.

While in Maryland, I listened to the Senators games on WTOP; their announcer, Dan Daniels, called a good game, and it was a kick hearing a voice that was different from By Saam's. Plus, I got the Phillies scores from time to time. Mom called twice to update me on the pennant race, and, of course, I scanned the boxes in the *Evening Star*, the conservative alternative to the *Washington Post*. Grams refused to read the *Post*.

Porky, a large collie shepherd mix, bounded toward us, followed by decrepit Mutt and Elsie.

"Well, who do we have here?" Jimmy said.

"They both did their pop!" Elsie called out excitedly.

I looked at her strangely. Did she know she had ruined Rice Krispies for me? Why did she find it necessary to broadcast bowel movements? I never heard Dan Daniels do it.

Chuck Hinton steps in—the leftfielder hitting .274 and 2 for 3 today. Here's the pitch. Fastball. Hinton tags it! Into the right field gap between Demeter and Thomas!

Demeter picks it up and fires to Don Wert at third. Too late! Hinton with a stand-up triple! Wow! Hinton was a racehorse around those bases. Must've really done his pop today!

"Let's go listen to Moms," Elsie pronounced.

Now, *that* was something I liked.

That Elsie had introduced me to a *comedian* was refreshing. The books she read seemed archaic. The furniture in her house was dowdy and made even more so by doilies, throws, and ugly vases. Several dark aquariums didn't help. I came to feel that she embraced fads and prevailing pop culture as a bridge to my sisters and me. So I was overjoyed when she pulled out the comedy records. That she never *spoke* the words "POP culture" was another plus.

Moms Mabley was a 70-year-old African American who had toured for decades on what was called the "chitlin' circuit," akin to the Negro Leagues of baseball. She was now producing albums for wider audiences, and Elsie had latched onto her with gusto. My only exposure to professional comedians was our Smothers Brothers albums, sitcom characters, and an occasional stand-up on the Ed Sullivan Show.

We laughed at Moms' visit to the United Nations on one record and at her taking on Khrushchev in Geneva on another. "John and Jackie" had sent her there to warn the fool.

One nugget of Moms wisdom I never forgot: "Do what you want to do. But know what you're doing!" Even Dad hadn't offered that from his bag of Daddisms. That is not a criticism of Dad, because he told me "if you can't say anything nice about somebody, don't say anything at all."

Moms had a gleeful and mischievous style, even laughing while she delivered her surprise:

"I got on a bus and sat next to this old man who was drinking whiskey. Drinking whiskey right on the bus. I said, 'Don't you know you're going to hell?' He said, 'Well, you might as well have a drink, too, because we're on the same bus!'"

As I grew older, my favorite bits became her tragicomic unmasking of racism in the Deep South, including the Sam Jones classic:

"This guy died and went up to The Gate. St. Peter says, 'Who are you?' He says, 'I'm Sam Jones!' St. Peter looks in the book and says, 'We got no Sam Jones.' He says, 'Come on. You know me. Look in the book again.' St. Peter looks in the book again and says, 'We ain't got no Sam Jones.' He says, 'You know me! I'm the cat that married that white girl on the Capitol steps in Jackson, Mississippi!' St. Peter says, 'How long was that?' He says, 'About five minutes ago.'"

Familial segregation seemed to be the norm on my visits here. Out of doors I hung mostly with Jimmy, working in the garden or learning the riding mower. Elsie and I bonded over fun and learning. Grams was a whole different ballgame. She was in many ways the most loving grandmother. She sat with me when I was sick. I spent hours next to her on the piano bench, entertained by her mastery of the keys and grateful for her patience in teaching me chords and hand posture. She alone affirmed that I *did* have musical aptitude. Together we watched *Perry Mason* and *Bonanza* and *The Beverly Hillbillies*.

But when her life was subsumed by religion or ideology, it was bonkers.

She watched *The Virginian* because its star, James Drury, was "a good conservative." The *Real McCoys* received her blessing since lead Walter Brennan was currently campaigning for Barry Goldwater. She seemed to have a mental checklist of anyone who supported JFK in 1960. She would not watch *The Joey Bishop Show*. Frank Sinatra was off limits. Elsie told me she once walked out of the room when Tony Curtis appeared on *What's My Line?*

The next day, Sunday, I found myself in her room, which featured polished and flawless mahogany furniture from the 1920s: four-poster bed, nightstand, high dresser, and vanity. On the latter was a framed photo of my grandfather, who had died 34 years before. In white tie, he was fabulously handsome with a suitable baldness, proud eyes, and mouth creased ever so slightly with flight of fancy.

Grams followed my eyes.

"How he would have loved you!"

"I'm sorry he died."

"I was blessed for as long as he lived. No man could match him, and that is why I never remarried."

Two others were on display, though. A postcard-size portrait of Jesus, his golden locks flowing, leaned against her mirror. It had replaced the paint-by-number savior from the old house, which I later found in a cardboard box in the basement next to a beat-up game of Tiddlywinks. And Grams wore a jeweled "Barry" pin.

"Are those diamonds?" I asked.

Grams laughed. "Oh, no. These are white rhinestones. They simulate diamonds."

"Mom is for Goldwater."

"Of course," she approved. "Your mother was brought up correctly."

She paused and then launched into campaign "issues."

"You know, there's this idea going around that Goldwater is Jewish. It is true that his grandfather was a Jewish immigrant from Poland named 'Goldwasser,' and his father was also Jewish. Now all of that is fine, and they were prosperous merchants in Arizona. But Barry's *mother* was Episcopalian—not Catholic, thank goodness—and he was raised in her faith. So," she continued with emphasis, "he is a *Christian*."

I took it in for a second.

"Does he like baseball?"

Grams laughed. "Well, I assume so. He is a man and he celebrates everything that is American."

"That's good," I said. "The Phillies beat the Giants yesterday, and we're 30 games over .500!"

"As I told you, the statistics will help with your mathematics."

"Jim Bunning won his 16th game and lowered his ERA to 2.23. That's the average number of earned runs he's given up per nine innings. Also, Gus Triandos hit a grand slam. That's a home run with the bases loaded."

She smiled. "Who are your favorite players?"

"I have four. Cookie Rojas, Johnny Callison, Richie Allen, and Chris Short."

I ran out to get my Phillies yearbook. When I returned, I showed her their write-ups and photos; as she saw Allen, her lips creased.

"I don't know," she sighed. "Don't you think the Negroes were better off in their own leagues?"

I froze. Then she said it.

"If God had wanted white people and black people to associate, he would have made us the same color."

It did not compute. The Phillies wouldn't be the Phillies without Richie Allen. Of course, I had heard this talk in angry rumblings on the news or occasionally from the mouths of strangers, but never from a member of my family. I said nothing but didn't want to share baseball with her after that.

I walked into the kitchen where Elsie stood at the toaster with a runaway smile.

"I have a treat for you!"

"What?"

"I got them at the store. They're brand new!"

The toaster ejected its treasure to Elsie's delight. "Pop-Tarts!"

ANGRY FASTBALL

National League Standings Morning of September 30, 1964				
TEAM	WINS	LOSSES	PCT.	G.B.
Cincinnati	91	67	.576	--
St. Louis	91	67	.576	--
Philadelphia	90	69	.566	1.5
San Francisco	87	70	.554	3.5
Milwaukee	83	73	.532	7
Pittsburgh	78	78	.500	12
Los Angeles	77	80	.490	13.5
Chicago	73	84	.465	17.5
Houston	65	92	.414	25.5
New York	51	106	.325	39.5

Issues in school on this Wednesday took precedence over baseball woes. My forward rolls in gym class were so ungainly that I began to fear another "Lead Bottom" nickname. I heard the snickers. How soon would I become "Acrobutt" or worse? Another clumsy kid had gotten a doctor's note to get out of phys ed entirely, but that seemed a humiliation too far.

Chorus was a second minefield. Miss de Krafft had begun rehearsing us for a winter concert, which included such breezy offerings as "Sleigh Ride" and "There's a Hole in My Bucket." The trouble began with the selection, "If You Can't Sing, Whistle." I could not whistle. I had been faking it for days. Every time Claire de Krafft eyed me, I was sure she would call me out. Feeding my panic was the suspicion that she had overheard Mike Murphy and me mocking her as "Claire de Loon."

Betty Lou Brown and Dave Hibbard and other pure talents belted out the lyrics and whistled up a storm while I was a sweaty mess.

"Are you getting good exercise in gym?" Mom asked me.

"No. But I've lost a couple of pounds in chorus."

The words to the song bothered me, too. There was a line about birds not being able to sing so they *just whistle*. Even they could outperform me. I half expected Miss de Krafft to replace me with a four-inch willow tit. Plus, since March, I was upset with birds in general.

On the Jennings School playground, in sixth grade, a tetherball slammed into my right little finger, bent it back and broke it. A teacher told me to head home. On the way I kept working it in and out of joint; the pain increased until, steps from our house, I passed out under a tree. When I came to, I looked up—and a bird crapped right on my face.

It was my worst day in New Jersey.

"Your Mom said this broken finger is 'for the birds,'" said an attendant in the emergency room at West Jersey Hospital. He and the doctor and Mom laughed.

"Is it off my face?" I said, annoyed.

"It's all wiped off," Mom assured me to another round of chuckles.

When I started seventh grade at Haddon Township Junior-Senior High School, I had to make peace with its mascot, the hawk. Hawks and eagles are magnificent and beloved fliers, I told myself, not one of the little shitters that got me.

Miss de Krafft never embarrassed me, but my class clowning

earned me an "unsatisfactory" in conduct for her class. Comedy had a downside.

Tonight, I finished my homework and turned on the radio. The Phillies had to end this horror; Bunning had to salvage the final game of the three-game series in St. Louis. There had been fierce debate in the press about Mauch pitching Bunning and Short with insufficient rest; in our house, Mom, Linda, and I supported his strategy, while Dad did not. Either way, the bullpen wasn't helping much. We were still hitting well, but not enough and not in the right spots. And we weren't getting any breaks.

After six innings, I turned off the game and went to sleep. It was 8-0 Cards, and Curt Simmons was hurling a no-hitter. It was a real turn of the knife. Simmons had been a Phillies star for 13 seasons before the Cardinals signed him in 1960 as a free agent. In 1950, he was one of the "Whiz Kids" that propelled the Phils into the World Series. The trio of Simmons (17 wins), Robin Roberts (20 wins), and reliever Jim Konstanty (16 wins, 22 saves, 2.66 ERA as the National League MVP) was the ride to glory.

"He might have won 20 that year," Aunt Nelle tutored me, "but he was called to active duty in September. That war in Korea robbed us! With Simmons, we might even have won the Series against the Yanks."

With only two pennants, in 1915 and 1950, Phillies heroes were few and far between. That one of them was now sealing our coffin stunk like the wastewater and dead fish of the Delaware River.

The next day, the Phillies were off. It was of no consequence that they put five runs on the board during the final three frames. The 8-5 loss was our tenth in a row.

Conversations among my classmates had moved on from the Phillies to hallway hearsay and Hurricane Hilda, a monster storm that was bearing down on New Orleans. In science class, Mr. Zoranski drew a blackboard diagram of how hurricanes formed. I liked his animated drawing.

"Hot air rises! The warm, moist air over the ocean rises, and new air fills the vacuum. *That* air heats up and also rises. A swirling starts. The warm, moist air that has moved up starts to form clouds. Soon the whole system rotates faster and faster until you have a massive cyclone! Hilda's winds are now 150 miles per hour!"

By the time he was done, I figured people in New Orleans had worse problems than Phillies fans. And I suspected Dad didn't know about this "hot air rising" thing, or else he wouldn't have made me help him put down floorboards in the attic in summer. Why couldn't we do attic work in December and put up Christmas lights in August instead of on the coldest day of the year? I thought about inviting Mr. Zoranski to our house for a sit-down with Dad.

At home, Mom was peeved with poll results that showed Goldwater lagging behind LBJ.

"I don't believe a word of it!" she fumed. "Gallup never called *me*."

When the paper came, I read Sandy Grady's column. And it made me angry.

"Basically, Gene Mauch had tried a magnificent heist—a steal of a pennant with two solid players (Allen and Callison) and two pitchers (Bunning and Short). As Stan Musial said at 11 o'clock: 'I know it's tough on people in Philadelphia to lose like this—but all year, the pros in the league felt the Phils had the talent of a third or fourth team. Gee, Mauch almost got away with it.'"

We had plenty of "solid players." Alex Johnson was batting .305. Rojas was at .296. Taylor had 139 hits. Gonzalez had the best fielding percentage in the league. Bennett and Mahaffey and Culp were no Cy Young candidates, but they did combine for more than a third of our wins. We were a first place team for most of the season, and we deserved to be. It was crappy that Musial was kicking us when we were down and that Grady was buying into it.

Shortly after Dad got home, he and Mom got into another squabble about the tailspin.

"Mauch should have given Bunning a rest. He could have started Baldschun or Roebuck or another bullpen pitcher."

"You're just piling on."

"Well, tell me how *you'd* fix it."

"If I could fix it, I'd be on the club's payroll."

"That's another thing," Dad raised his voice. "The front office should have picked up some veteran players as insurance."

"They got Frank Thomas in August!" Mom raised her voice in return. "He's the extra bat we needed against left-handers."

"Until he broke his thumb," Dad fumed.

"He wasn't out that long."

"He broke his thumb," Dad insisted. "We're bedeviled!"

"That happened *before* Chico Ruiz. You said the curse started *then*."

Mom had taunted Dad. His face was red, and I knew they had reached critical mass.

I held up the phone receiver from the kitchen to quash it with levity.

"Mom, it's for you. It's Mr. Gallup!"

Mom wasn't having it.

"That's not funny," she barked. "Not everything is a joke."

Dad slammed down the paper and went upstairs. Mom took the receiver from my hand and hung it up. She ripped some pots and pans from the cupboard to start dinner.

Comedy had failed. And I felt humiliated.

I took my ball and glove and walked outside. I threw an angry fastball against the garage door. Then another. The third one cracked a panel on the door.

Great. Now I'd be punished for that.

I took off my glove and slammed it to the ground. After a few seconds, I kicked the glove into the back yard and leaned up against a tree.

Looking back, I'm grateful a bird didn't shit on me.

BEFORE THE FALL

On Sunday, September 20, Pastor Paules tapped into the World Series euphoria to deliver a sermon, "God Throws Out the First Pitch." As we left, I asked Mom, "Will President Johnson throw out the first pitch?"

"If Johnson comes to the stadium," Mom stood firm, "Goldwater should be invited, too. Equal time."

"Goldwater would throw high and right," Linda said.

"Cute," Mom said reproachfully. "We'll see at the 1965 World Series."

After church I grabbed my basketball and headed to a two-hoop court a few blocks from home. Another kid was there, and after noticing that he was as bad a shooter as I was, I offered a one-on-one. He was wearing a beat-up red jacket; on it was a white felt "P" that had been sewn on slightly crooked. Miss after miss, we had the best time. With each clumsy dribble we laughed more. There was little talk, no winner, only some unexplained sweetness as free as the sky.

That afternoon in Los Angeles, the Phillies beat the Dodgers, 3-2. It was our 90th win. Tomorrow night I would be at Connie Mack Stadium with Dad and Linda to watch Art Mahaffey go for number 91. Who doubted that our lead was insurmountable?

Mom walked into my room to say goodnight as my radio, tuned to Wibbage, blared "The House of the Rising Sun."

And it's been the ruin of many a poor boy
And God I know I'm one.

"Is that the Beatles again?"

"No. The Animals. I like the song."

"I know. You and Linda keep singing it."

"What's up with the house in New Orleans?" I wondered. "Why does it ruin people?"

Mom did not want to answer.

"Mafia?"

"Oh, for heaven's sake."

"Then what?"

Mom opened my bureau drawer. "Have you packed your gym bag for tomorrow?"

"Not yet. You're not telling me about the house."

She took my white socks and Hawk T-shirt from the drawer and put them in my gym bag.

"If it's not the Mafia, what is it?"

"All right," Mom turned around and gestured with her right hand. "It's a place where men pay women for S-E-X."

In her hand, by unhappy circumstance, was my jockstrap. I stared at it, paralyzed. Mom looked at it and locked up. For too many seconds we were frozen in awkward apocalypse.

Mom jammed the licentious pouch into my gym bag and made her escape.

"Come right home from school so you can do your homework before the game."

"I will. I will."

I heard Mom pedal it downstairs as if the Politburo were after her. I sat on my bed, heart pounding. Wibbage played "Under the

Boardwalk," but I had no interest in finding out what went on there.

Yes, I'd be at the game tomorrow. Baseball was not only the antidote to mortifying moments with Mom, but for the tension that roiled our house before the Phillies took off. Life was good. Nine months before, in this room, I had read that the Dodgers were odds-on favorites to win the 1964 pennant. Now the Dodgers were 75-75 and the Phillies were 90-60. I went to sleep knowing dreams could happen.

The next morning I came down early for breakfast. The aroma of scrapple hustled me into the kitchen. Scrapple was my favorite morning fare. Liver pudding was a close second, and later in life I would engage in debates about the difference between the two. Basically, they are "parts" left over from butchering. Liver pudding is spicier, fried up like a mush that I would eagerly pile onto toast. Scrapple is thinly sliced from a loaf, browned and served with syrup. Unknowingly, I was a major fan of hog offal.

WCAU Radio was on, volume low, and Mom stood at the stove murdering a pan of already-too-brown scrambled eggs.

"Two thousand fans showed up at the airport!" she said excitedly.

"Wow!"

"Everyone says they'll wrap it up by the weekend."

I sat and gulped my juice. Upstairs, I heard one of my sisters enter the bathroom with Diana Ross on full blast: *"But all you do is treat me bad, Break my heart and leave me sad..."* Under the table, Duchess waited patiently for the chewy eggs I would invariably offer.

Mom spun around with a smile and a one-candled cupcake. I had forgotten it was September 21.

"Happy Half Birthday!"

I blew out the candle with a confident wish.

"It *will* come true," I insisted.

"Hope so," Mom said.

HOPE

	Pennant Race Morning of October 2, 1964			
TEAM	**WINS**	**LOSSES**	**PCT.**	**G.B.**
St. Louis	92	67	.579	--
Cincinnati	92	68	.575	.5
Philadelphia	90	70	.563	2.5

Dad sat in his recliner reading *The Power of Positive Thinking*.

"Are you going to listen to the game?" I asked.

"No," he replied.

Mom signaled that I should step away from the grump.

He closed his eyes. "I'm visualizing a night when I don't have to hear the name Chico Ruiz."

"How's that going?" Mom half-mocked.

"Not well," he replied, slamming shut the book.

The idea that Ruiz's steal of home had cursed us had taken hold in Philadelphia. Dad's premonition was now on the lips of scores of fans. A date with the Reds at Crosley Field tonight only exacerbated the handwringing.

"I looked up his birthday," Mom said. "He's a Sagittarius."

"What does that mean?" Dad asked.

"He's impatient. He's careless. That's why he ran without a sign."

"Johnson should send him back to Cuba," Dad piled on.

"Should I write to the White House?" I asked.

"No more letters to Johnson!" Mom insisted.

"So no one's listening to the game?"

"I *may* listen," Mom offered from the sofa.

"I'm going to watch TV," Dad declared. "This *Addams Family* is a funny show. There's nothing funny about Chico Ruiz."

Mom decreed. "Worst Cuban since Castro."

At 10:15 p.m. I was alone in my room when the malevolent Sagittarius keyed a two-run sixth to make it 3-0 Reds. The Phils had turned a triple play in the fourth, but our bats stayed silent. Cincy's Jim O'Toole took a shutout into the eighth. We were six outs away from elimination, and for the first time, I realized it was *goodbye Phillies for 1964*. When Bobby Wine flied out to right, I felt a shiver go through me. How could this have happened?

I was half-listening to the broadcast when Frank Thomas reached first on a pop-up mishandled by Reds shortstop Leo Cardenas. Johnny Briggs pinch-ran. Cookie Rojas walked, moving Briggs to second. Tony Taylor singled to center, scoring Briggs and advancing Rojas to third. It was 3-1 Reds, but I had been lured into this air castle before, so I plunged into a science fiction paperback.

In a universe far away, Reds reliever Billy McCool replaced O'Toole and Richie Allen tripled to right, scoring Rojas and Taylor. It was tied, 3-3.

What?

It was tied, 3-3.

Before I could process it, Alex Johnson singled up the middle, scoring Allen.

I scrambled out the door and down to the living room where Mom was hugging the radio. Dad had already sped there from the family room.

"We're ahead!" I cheered.

"Allen hit a triple?" Dad asked.

"Allen hit a triple, and Johnson singled in the go-ahead run," I reported.

"Short hit Cardenas with a pitch in the seventh and Cardenas charged him with a bat!" Mom added. "That got us revved up."

Linda came down. "I can't believe it!"

The game moved to the bottom of the eighth. We *led*, 4-3.

"Six more outs," Mom said. "Who's up for the Reds?"

"They'll probably pinch-hit for Ellis," I answered. "Then Pete Rose and—"

"And?" Dad asked.

"Chico Ruiz."

Dad threw up his hands and headed back to the family room.

Mauch turned the ball over to Jack Baldschun who would go for his 21st save. His ERA had ballooned from 2.30 in 1963 to a still-respectable 3.12 this year, but his signature screwball, which he could break left or right depending on the hitter, still fooled a legion of batters. His arsenal also included a sinking fastball, curve, and slider.

In the bottom of the eighth, he struck out pinch hitter Johnny Edwards and forced Rose and Ruiz to ground out.

"It's safe to come up!" Linda yelled down to Dad.

"He got Ruiz?" Dad said as he hustled in.

"On a grounder," I replied.

"Baldschun keeps his screwball low," Dad explained. "I *said* Mauch should have used him more."

Mom rolled her eyes.

The bottom of the ninth was Jack at his best. Vada Pinson grounded to short. Frank Robinson grounded to short. Deron Johnson struck out. One, two, three, and our 10-game nightmare was history.

"Wow. Just—wow," Dad said, bemused.

"Pinch me!" Mom said.

She got out the popcorn maker, and it popped to the chitchat of victory. Mom looked so happy you'd think East Berlin had fallen. Soon there was more good news via By Saam: "In an old-fashioned pitchers' duel, Al Jackson has outlasted Bob Gibson, and the Mets beat the Cardinals, 1-0."

"The *Mets* beat the Cardinals!" Dad whooped. "Can you believe it?"

By Saam continued, "It's Jackson's 11th win of the year for the Mets and his third shutout. Gibson, who pitched eight innings, falls to 18-12."

"Can you believe it?" Dad repeated.

"We're still alive!" Linda proclaimed.

And I *felt* alive on this Friday night in October. Maybe the losing streak was a test of our resilience. Maybe we were destined for triumph after all. How else to explain the 51-108 Mets defeating the 92-67 Cardinals—in St. Louis?

The Phillies were off on Saturday, but for us to stay in contention, the Mets had to beat the Cardinals again. It was the "Game of the Week" on ABC, and we were front and center in the family room. On paper, it looked to be a rout: Ray Sadecki going for his 21st win versus "Fat Jack" Fisher who had already dropped 17 for the cellar dwellers. Fat Jack was known for serving up history-making swats: in 1960 to Ted Williams in his final at-bat; in 1961 to Roger Maris for his 60th, to tie Babe Ruth; and this year to Willie Stargell, the first home run in Shea Stadium.

In the top of the first, though, it was Sadecki who had bad stuff: He gave up four singles and threw a wild pitch. Fat Jack took the mound with a 4-0 lead. The right-hander got Curt Flood, but then the real flood began. Lou Brock walked. Bill White homered. Ken Boyer homered. Dick Groat doubled. Dad buried his head in his hands and moaned.

"This guy sells more Alka-Seltzer in New York than McCann Erickson," he said.

"Who's McCann Erickson?" I asked.

"It's an advertising company," Mom replied.

"Ginger wants to do advertising," I said.

"Let's hope she survives The Catholic," Mom answered.

"Let's hope we survive this inning," Dad emphasized.

The Mets led 4-3 after the first, and both starters hit the showers. From then on, in this craziest of seasons, it was ALL METS! THE BEASTS OF THE BASEMENT! Seven *more* Cardinals hurlers could not stop them. A six spot in the seventh made it 15-4, as we cheered every hit, every RBI.

"Unbelievable!" Linda said.

"Who doesn't love the Mets?" Mom offered.

"Mets fans," I joked.

The next day, Sunday, would be the final day of the regular season. And with it came the possibility of something that had *never happened* in the history of major league baseball.

Pennant Race Morning of October 4, 1964				
TEAM	WINS	LOSSES	PCT.	G.B.
St. Louis	92	69	.571	--
Cincinnati	92	69	.571	--
Philadelphia	91	70	.565	1

A three-way tie!

If the Phillies beat the Reds today and the Mets beat the Cardinals, Philadelphia, Cincinnati, and St. Louis would end up with identical records of 92-70. The National League had already announced a possible round robin to determine the champion. Home field was determined after each team drew straws.

On Monday, Cincinnati would play at Philadelphia; on Tuesday, St. Louis would play at Cincinnati; on Wednesday, Philadelphia would play at St. Louis. If a second round robin were needed, teams would draws straws again.

After a devastating two weeks, hope was in the air. In the vestibule at church, as I readied to light candles, I accosted Pastor Paules.

"Are you excited?"

"Yes," he said. "Tiger tails are on sale at PJ's for 39 cents."

"No! Didn't you see the sports page?"

"Ugh. Penn State fumbled nine times yesterday."

"No! The Phillies!"

"Oh," he said mischievously. "Are they playing today?"

Like the Sunday before, Pastor Paules led a prayer for the team. Yet his sermon indicated we could not always understand God's plans. He had read in the paper that a young woman from Philadelphia was on her first trip to Paris, sightseeing at Notre Dame Cathedral. A suicidal woman jumped from the church's tower and fell on the tourist, killing them both.

We drove home under dark, cloudy skies.

"What a sad story," Mom said. "How can you make sense of it?"

"We're not supposed to," Dad said.

"But still," she said shaking her head. "Why did the innocent girl have to die?"

Dad sighed. Then after a beat, "Sometimes you are just sitting there enjoying a baseball game and suddenly—"

"Chico Ruiz steals home!" Linda and I chimed in.

"That's right," Dad insisted. "With *Frank Robinson* up!"

"Pastor Paules says tiger tails are on sale at Penn Jersey."

"That's some marketing genius right there," Dad said. "Esso creates the slogan 'A Tiger in Your Tank.' Then they sell tiger tails for your gas cap so *you do their advertising for them!*"

"God works in mysterious ways," Linda said.

"Let's hope he's a Phillies fan," I said.

"We deserve the pennant," Mom insisted. "That's the only way this season makes sense." She paused. "This year. It had to *mean something*."

The game was on Channel 6 at 2:30. It was Jim Bunning (18-8) against John Tsitouris (9-12).

"Bunning is starting for the fourth time in nine games," Dad said. "Does he have anything left?"

"He *has* to," I said.

And he did.

He came out strong, mastering the Reds. And our bats exploded. In the third, a double by Richie Allen and singles by Wes Covington and Tony Taylor made it 3-0. Allen added a solo homer in the fifth.

In St. Louis during the top of the fifth, the Mets took the lead, 3-2.

In the sixth, the Phils decimated Cincinnati reliever Joey Jay. We were out of our seats on every hit, pumping our fists. It seemed the same primal force with which I pounded the garage door four days earlier.

Clay Dalrymple singled. Bobby Wine singled. Jim Bunning singled. Tony Gonzalez singled. Richie Allen homered again.

It was 9-0. The team was making a statement. We went up 10-0 in the seventh on the way to pummeling seven Reds pitchers. Bunning finished off a six-hit shutout in a breezy 2 hours and 28 minutes.

"People got on Mauch for pitching Bunning and Short so often," Mom said. "But Short was decent yesterday and Bunning was phenomenal today."

"No one should blame Mauch," Linda echoed.

The game in St. Louis lagged behind ours. And the news turned sour as the Cards led 8-4 after six.

"Please, Casey. Get the Mets going," Mom prayed.

"They have to come back," I prayed with her.

We waited.

With each update, the final puzzle piece receded farther from our grasp. St. Louis tacked on three more in the bottom of the eighth with Bob Gibson in charge in relief. The final came like a thunderbolt. 11-5. The Cardinals were National League champions. The Phillies and Reds tied for second place, one game behind.

We sat in the family room for what seemed like forever. Linda left. Mom started to cry and then sobbed. I held back tears.

It was over.

It was really over.

Mom got up and consoled herself as she walked away. "At least Goldwater will win."

After a beat, I turned to Dad with one last stab at humor. "Mom is in for a rough year."

It worked. Dad smiled, let out a chuckle and tousled my hair. After another prolonged silence, he summoned some ancient wisdom.

"Next year," he said.

EPILOGUE

"Next year" never came.

In the off-season, the Phillies acquired two name players, first baseman Dick Stuart and pitcher Bo Belinsky. Stuart ended up with 28 homers and 95 RBIs, but batted only .234. Belinsky toiled in the bullpen, going 4-9 with a 4.84 ERA. Allen and Callison and Rojas continued to shine, while Bunning notched 19 wins and Short racked up 18. But the rest of the pitching staff was mediocre. We went 85-76 and finished sixth.

Ma-HEY-fey fought a sore arm for two wins, and after the Phils dealt him, Aunt Nelle claimed to have done a cartwheel on the capitol grounds in Harrisburg. The trade was a blockbuster: Mahaffey, Alex Johnson, and catcher Pat Corrales to the Cardinals in exchange for Bill White, Dick Groat, and Bob Uecker. Hopes for 1966 were sky-high when *Sports Illustrated* featured Groat on its cover under the heading, "Dick Groat and the New Phils." A *Sports Illustrated* cover surely meant good things.

White delivered with 103 RBIs and Groat chipped in with 152 hits, but Callison's production tailed off. Allen stayed hot with a .317 average, 40 homers, and 110 RBIs. Bunning, Short, and newcomer Larry Jackson combined for 54 wins, but, again, the bullpen was abysmal. Our 87-75 ledger was good for only fourth place.

There were individual achievements. To Dad's delight, Allen was voted to the All-Star squad in 1965, batting cleanup and collecting a hit in the NL's 6-5 win. And in a brilliant performance, Short fanned *18* Mets in one 15-inning affair. But the Phils had become yesterday's news. In 1967, fifth place; in 1968, seventh place; in 1969, fifth place in the NL East, 37 back of the Miracle Mets. In '71, '72, and '73, we were last-place jokes.

In 1968, Bunning was traded to Pittsburgh. Allen got into a nasty dispute with management and had continual run-ins with Mauch. The fans and press rode Allen hard. During the season, Mauch was fired. Callison's power faded and he was traded to the Cubs after 1969. Allen and Rojas were sent to St. Louis, and Allen said "good riddance" to the City of Brotherly Love. Short suffered back problems and was released in 1972.

All of my favorite Phillies were gone.

Through it all I remained steadfast. At home I followed every game; in college I checked the boxes every morning.

"1964" became a symbol for the city's poor sports fortunes; the unparalleled collapse was analyzed, over-analyzed, debated and written about for years. It messed with a lot of people who clung to a deep feeling of betrayal or hurt. Perhaps Dad, the psychic Cancer, did have a premonition. No doubt the Phils had an awful run of luck just as the Reds and Cardinals got hot. Likely, it was the breaks of the game.

The 1964 Phillies, though, had forever won my heart. Baseball was new to me then, as I cheered Ruben Amaro's Gold Glove play at Connie Mack or tried to imitate Richie Allen on a scruffy field in Oaklyn. "Wes Covington, Tony Gonzalez, and Johnny Callison" would always be my outfield. No one would ever throw a better screwball than Jack Baldschun. If they finished in second place, they also gave me enough thrills for a lifetime. They were the team of my youth.

On October 21, 1980, I was 27, and my youth seemed long gone.

Taffy died from kidney failure in 1975, and Duchess succumbed to old age soon after. We were all gone from home, so Mom had to go alone to have them put down. She cried for days. It was one of the great regrets of my life that I wasn't there to give them one last hug.

Ginger married Tom. She went to work for a small ad agency where, among other projects, she designed the sign for Freddy's Liquor Store on Cuthbert Boulevard. Whenever I passed Freddy's, I told anyone within earshot that my big sister created the sign. I never went into the store, but I once saw two nuns carrying out a carton of booze, and it cracked me up. I became an uncle when Tommy and Amy were born. In 1974, Ginger started her own ad agency, Donohue & Company; she was featured in *Philadelphia Magazine* as "One of the 76 People to Watch in 1976," the prelude to a long and successful marketing career. Grams never knew that she got her undergraduate degree from St. Joseph's University, a hotbed of Jesuits.

Linda was a math major at Wagner College on Staten Island, where she received her Bachelor of Science, cum laude. Her graduation gift was a Plymouth Duster. She worked for a while at Mayor Rohrer's bank, before being hired by a financial conglomerate where she excelled in top management and was never again "poor Linda." She dropped her dream of wedding a horse, married Bill Hetrick, and gave birth to Billy and Laura.

I loved my nieces and nephews, but Tommy, Amy, Billy, and Laura continued our family history of boring, Anglo names, except for the two weeks when I was Wikfsihn.

Susan was Phi Beta Kappa in college, the foundation for a 30-year career in public service.

When I was in high school, Dad pulled some strings with the mayor and got Nana an apartment in the new William G. Rohrer Towers, a senior citizen complex in Westmont. I was jealous that she lived in a section of Haddon Township that had its own ZIP code. In 1975, Nana suffered a stroke, a heart attack, and a second stroke that took her speech. As she lay in West Jersey Hospital, Mom was one floor above being prepped for a breast biopsy. Later, Nana asked for the news with her eyes, and Mom answered that the lump was benign. Unable to smile, she squeezed Mom's hand. The next day, she died.

Aunt Vicki died of esophageal cancer in 1967. It was hard on Aunt Nelle—especially when she had the gout—but in time she regained her form. In college I grew a beard, and she mockingly called me "Abe." It was a mistake to try to debate her.

"You're okay with Lincoln's beard."

"Lincoln wasn't a hippie!"

"I'm not a hippie."

"You look like one. Why don't you move to Oakland and play for Charley Finley's freaks?"

At 93, Aunt Nelle moved into a nursing home in the shadow of Three Mile Island. The next year, there was the big meltdown. She asked that a typewriter be brought to her bed so she could punch out a letter "to the dumb-bells at that place who are trying to kill me in my prime."

My beard was small fish compared to *the Catholic matter*. After Ginger married Tom, Grams refused to see or speak to her for seven years. The breakthrough came after Tommy was born in 1972.

"Come down to Maryland!" Aunt Elsie told Ginger. "We'd love to see you and the baby. No telling if Grams will come out of her room."

Grams remained sequestered. At last, she peered out of her bedroom and made her way down the hall to where we were gathered. The instant she saw Tommy, she melted. "That gorgeous red hair," she whispered, cradling him. There was palpable relief that Grams had once again embraced Ginger. Then she saw my "McGovern" button, nearly choked, and headed back to her cell.

Six months from now, in 1981, Aunt Nelle and Grams would pass away within three weeks of each other. Aunt Nelle was buried in Middletown beside her companion, Victoria Kavanaugh. Grams rested in Mt. Lebanon next to her husband, Arthur Grove Forster. After everyone left the graveside, I said a sweet goodbye. Then I tossed 60 cents onto her coffin—a Kennedy half-dollar and a Roosevelt dime.

Mom's interest in astrology blossomed into a career. She took an astrology course and soon was teaching it herself. She wrote feature articles for *American Astrology* magazine, interpreting the charts of newsmakers and celebrities. As far as I know, she never did Eisenhower's horoscope to find out why he stole the nomination from Bob Taft. Two years from now, she would begin writing the magazine's "Daily Guides," which, because of their humor and insight, would remain popular for decades.

In 1969, Dad received some calls from a man who claimed to be his father. He hung up, deeming it a prank. But he confronted Nana, who came clean. She said she thought it would be easier to tell him his father had died than to tell the truth: His father had taken off. When the next call came, a rendezvous was set; it would be after Dad's nighttime Army Reserve meeting in Camden. My father was 52, and life had assigned him the task of sitting in his car on a dark street and waiting for a tap on the window from the man who gave him life, yet chose to know nothing of it.

The encounter was filled with every emotion you'd expect, even before the news that Louis Wolfsohn was dying. Eventually, stories were swapped, holes were filled in; Dad learned he had a half-brother who was a doctor in Philadelphia. My grandfather died before I laid eyes on him, but I had seen him all my life in my own father's resolve to make a home and love his children.

In 1979, Mom and Dad had a house built in Satellite Beach, Florida, less than a mile from the Atlantic. They picked the spot, south of Cape Canaveral, because it was near Patrick Air Force Base where Dad would have military privileges and because it was an area, they were told, where hurricanes rarely hit. I helped them move, and *the day we got there*, Hurricane David came ashore. We were ordered to evacuate to Melbourne, where we spent two days in a motel watching the world fly by. When we left, Dad packed the room towels. "They expect you to take them," he said. "They plan for that."

From seventh grade on, I did impressions of every teacher and bandied enough wit to fill up my yearbook with predictions that I would become a comedian.

I chose journalism as my field and was accepted by The University of Wisconsin. Mom thought the Madison campus was "too radical," so I headed to Lindsey Nelson's alma mater, The University of Tennessee. To Mom's chagrin, I became a liberal anyway.

In Knoxville, I penned a humor column for the UT *Daily Beacon* called "The Funnies," and won $5 in my dorm's talent contest for an imitation of a local grocer named Cas Walker, a crusty old sort who appeared in his own shoestring TV spots. The ads had worse production values than *Plan 9 From Outer Space*, as Cas threw down cards from an easel while shouting out the day's specials. He once pulled out a hanky and spent 20 of his 30 seconds blowing his nose before offering his cut-rate cabbage.

As an account executive at Holder, Kennedy & Company, a Nashville public relations firm, I often staged comedy slide shows at client meetings and once got in trouble with a Bible Belt CEO when I showed a photo of two humping polar bears. I wrote and performed in the city's annual "Gridiron Show," which raised money for journalism scholarships by skewering politicians. A rave review by Eugene Wyatt of *The Tennessean* encouraged me to head west, where I quickly became a regular at Mitzi Shore's Comedy Store in Hollywood. It was a remarkable place, filled with ingenious observers of the world. The nightly lineups included stars such as Robin Williams and Richard Pryor, plus up-and-comers Argus Hamilton, Cathy Ladman, Jim Carrey, Paul Mooney, and Arsenio Hall. As I readied for my first paid spot in the Original Room, Steve Martin showed up, went on before me and did 30 minutes. During my set, people rushed to get his autograph and the crowd listened to nothing I said.

"It'll make you stronger," Mitzi consoled me in her famous nasal whine.

I quickly honed my Mitzi impression and joined a non-exclusive club. Everybody did Mitzi. Taxi drivers and hookers on Sunset had her down. I met other Phillies fans, including a brilliant comic from Philadelphia named Larry Beezer. We sat in Ben Franks until three in the morning doing our By Saam impressions (his was better) and re-living the 1964 collapse.

Every second at "The Store" was an adrenaline rush, watching America's funniest (or most neurotic) people mine universal truths about subjects both mundane and taboo. Jimmie Walker observed:

"More violence in Northern Ireland. Protestants versus Catholics, Catholics versus Protestants. Just goes to show you—in a country with no Blacks, Jews, or Mexicans, people can improvise."

Another memorable stand-up, Harris Peet, talked about his matronly grade-school teacher.

"When you're a kid, you don't know what a lesbian is. You just think—My, she has nicer suits than my dad!"

I laughed, picturing Nelle and Vicki in their "smart jackets."

When I printed up my headshots, I decided to delete the pain-in-the-ass "h" in "Wolfsohn." For as long as I did comedy, I would be "Carl Wolfson." I could not have dreamed I was on the threshold of a career that would take me around the world, a high-spirited journey of more than 8,000 performances on television and radio, and in the great comedy clubs of my generation.

All that lay ahead.

This day was about the Phillies.

Connie Mack had fallen to the wrecking ball, and the spotlight had moved to Veterans Stadium, a huge bowl in South Philly. By 1976, a new lineup—Steve Carlton, Mike Schmidt, Garry Maddox, Larry Bowa—led a resurgence. Under manager Danny Ozark, we won 101 games and dominated the East. In the NLCS, however, we lost to Cincinnati's Big Red Machine. In 1977, the Phils went 101-61 again, but fell to the Dodgers in the NLCS. They won a third division title in 1978, but again lost to the Dodgers.

Aunt Nelle wrote to me in a scrawl: "They can't seem to get by Brooklyn."

This year, Dallas Green, a bench warmer in 1964, was our new manager, and Pete Rose, who had bedeviled us as a young Red, was our first baseman. We won the East for the fourth time in five years and battled Houston in the NLCS. The five-game series became an instant classic, with *four* games going to extra innings. In the decider at the Astrodome, Nolan Ryan staked Houston to a 5-2 lead, but the Phillies exploded for five runs in the eighth. The Astros knotted it, 7-7. With two outs in the tenth, Gary Maddox doubled home Del Unser; then, Dick Ruthven shut down the Astros.

The Phils sprinted from their dugout—National League champs for the first time since 1950!

In the World Series we faced the Kansas City Royals, who had also won division titles in '76, '77, and '78 without advancing. It was the first time in Series history that two rookie managers, Dallas Green and Jim Frey, matched wits.

In Game One, the Phils trailed 4-0, before Bake McBride's three-run homer keyed a five-run third. We won, 7-6, in front of 65,000 delirious fans at The Vet. In Game Two, we erased a 4-2 Royals lead with four in the eighth for another thrilling come-from-behind victory. The Phillies were dubbed "The Cardiac Kids." During the second game, Kansas City's George Brett left with a nasty case of hemorrhoids and had minor surgery the next day. He may have been the only player in postseason history to sit out a game without actually sitting.

Game Three at Royals Stadium was another heart-stopper. In the bottom of the tenth, Willie Mays Aikens drove in the clincher as Kansas City prevailed, 4-3. He starred again in Game Four, belting two taters in KC's 5-3 triumph.

With the Series tied, Game Five was crucial. The Phils came to bat in the ninth inning, down 3-2. Mike Schmidt singled *off George Brett's glove*. Del Unser doubled him home to tie it. Unser took third on a bunt, and Manny Trillo singled *off Dan Quisenberry's glove* for the go-ahead run. It was the opposite of 1964: The ball was bouncing *our* way. The Phillies flew home with a three games to two lead, and Schmidt cut to the chase: "We have a tomorrow. The Royals do not."

On the day of Game Six, I awoke to a glorious sun. I let it shine on my face, content to absorb its warmth and eternalness. I was happy. I needed no premonition to tell me how this day would end.

I grabbed a coffee and opened the *Los Angeles Times* sports section to the brilliant Jim Murray, who was Ray Kelly and Sandy Grady rolled into one. His column was about the Royals' Willie Wilson, who led the American League with 230 hits and 133 runs but was a disappearing act in the Series. "The guy wearing his number," Murray wrote, "looks more like Woodrow than Willie Wilson."

The last paragraph made me smile:

"So, the Kansas City Royals are precariously perched over a small ledge today with one foot dangling in space because they mislaid Willie the Whippet someplace down the line."

I continued to grin as I read the news. Ronald Reagan criticized President Carter for "doing nothing" about the hostages in Iran. Carter chided Reagan for saying that *trees* cause pollution. In Grosse Pointe Park, Michigan, women were welcomed to the police station to reclaim their underwear after the arrest of a local "lingerie thief." It was going to be a good day for writing jokes. I plunged into it, honing my impressions of Reagan and Carter. Both had easy voices to mimic, but it was their body language, the full range of non-verbal quirks, that sold the bit. I had read Stanislavsky's *On the Art of the Stage* and knew I had to *be* Reagan or *be* Carter, the same way I was Mrs. Drysdale years before.

During a walk on the beach, I thought about Taffy dragging Mom's purse and Duchess playing Claude Drysdale and Nana's irrepressible smile and how Aunt Vicki told me there would always be baseball. I thought about my next set at The Comedy Store and wondered if I'd ever be as happy as I was playing Ed Sullivan on a coffee table.

That evening I sat alone in my apartment. Joe Garagiola, Tony Kubek, and Tom Seaver called the game on NBC, and I smiled as Carlton pitched a solid seven innings. Super Steve had won 24 games in the regular season and was going for his third win in the postseason. In the top of the ninth, with the Phillies leading 4-1 and the Royals down to their final out, I picked up the phone and dialed a number in Florida.

"Whooooo-hooooooooooo!" Dad answered.

I could hear Mom clapping in the background.

"Hi, Dad."

"I knew it was you!"

"Amazing," I said. "Do you see the police on horseback?"

"They're trying to keep the fans from running onto the field."

"Two strikes on Wilson," I reported.

"I see it. I see it," Dad said.

"The crowd will tell you what happens," Joe Garagiola said.

"I think this is it!" Mom called out.

It was all in my throat. I squeezed the phone and held on.

At 11:29 Eastern Time on October 21, 1980, reliever Tug McGraw hurled a pitch toward home plate.

It cut through the crisp air, traveling at the speed of redemption. It was a ball, of course, that Lead Bottom could never have hit. Its stitches were as beautiful as those drawn on a cupcake by a mother who sent her boy off to his game with a half-birthday kiss. It spun with the dreams of a father whose deepest wish was to share a World Series with his only son. It carried the hopes of a city that had waited too long and the memories of a family that had been made more whole by the spectacle of America's pastime.

It landed gently, on target, in Bob Boone's mitt, and for the first time in their 97-year history, the *Phillies* were the champions of baseball.

"We did it!" Mom cheered.

"Can you believe it?" Dad hollered. "Can you believe it?"

Fireworks exploded over a rocking Veterans Stadium, and I could see the three of us dancing under the fireworks of another night so many years ago.

"Yes," I answered, finally letting the tears flow. "I believe it."

Have a book idea?

Contact us at:

info@mascotbooks.com | www.mascotbooks.com